"Through her consummate research and a deep, abiding empathy with the characters which she has resurrected, Carole Wilkinson has that rare ability to bring the past to life, in all of its authentic, 'warts-and-all' realism. Recommended."
— *Magpies*

"Carole Wilkinson takes the reader beyond the surface of the Ned Kelly legend... She brings the story alive through the everyday life and struggles of this unlikely hero."
— *CBCA Book of the Year Judges' Report 2003*

"...a must-have if you are a Kelly Gang fanatic."
— *Joe Online*

Carole Wilkinson is an award-winning author of books for children. Her novel Dragonkeeper won the Children's Book Council of Australia's Book of the Year in 2004. She has a longstanding fascination with dragons and is interested in the history of everything. Carole is a meticulous researcher who finds it difficult to stop researching and begin writing. She once searched for weeks to find out whether there were daffodils in Han Dynasty China. Carole is married, has a daughter, and lives in inner-city Melbourne.

Find out about Carole's books on her website:
www.carolewilkinson.com.au

Ned Kelly was a thief, a bank robber and a murderer. He was in trouble with the law from the age of 12. He stole hundreds of horses and cattle. He robbed two banks. He killed three men. Yet, when Ned was sentenced to death, thousands of people rallied save his life. He stood up to the authorities and fought for what he believed in. He defended the rights of people who had no power.

Black Snake

THE DARING OF NED KELLY

FOR

John and Lili

Black Snake

THE DARING OF NED KELLY

Carole Wilkinson

WALKER BOOKS
AND SUBSIDIARIES
LONDON • BOSTON • SYDNEY • AUCKLAND

First published in 2002 by Black Dog Books
This edition published in 2019 by Walker Books Australia Ltd
Locked Bag 22, Newtown
NSW 2042 Australia
www.walkerbooks.com.au

EU Authorized Representative: HackettFlynn Ltd,
36 Cloch Choirneal, Balrothery, Co. Dublin, K32 C942, Ireland.
EU@walkerpublishinggroup.com

Cover designed by Blue Boat Design
Internal design by Guy Holt Design
Cover photograph: Mark Chew

A catalogue record for this book is available from the National Library of Australia

ISBN: 978 1 876372 93 4

Printed and bound in Australia by Griffin Press

The paper this book is printed on is certified against the Forest Stewardship Council® Standards. Griffin Press holds chain of custody certification SCS-COC-001185. FSC® promotes environmentally responsible, socially beneficial and economically viable management of the world's forests.

Contents

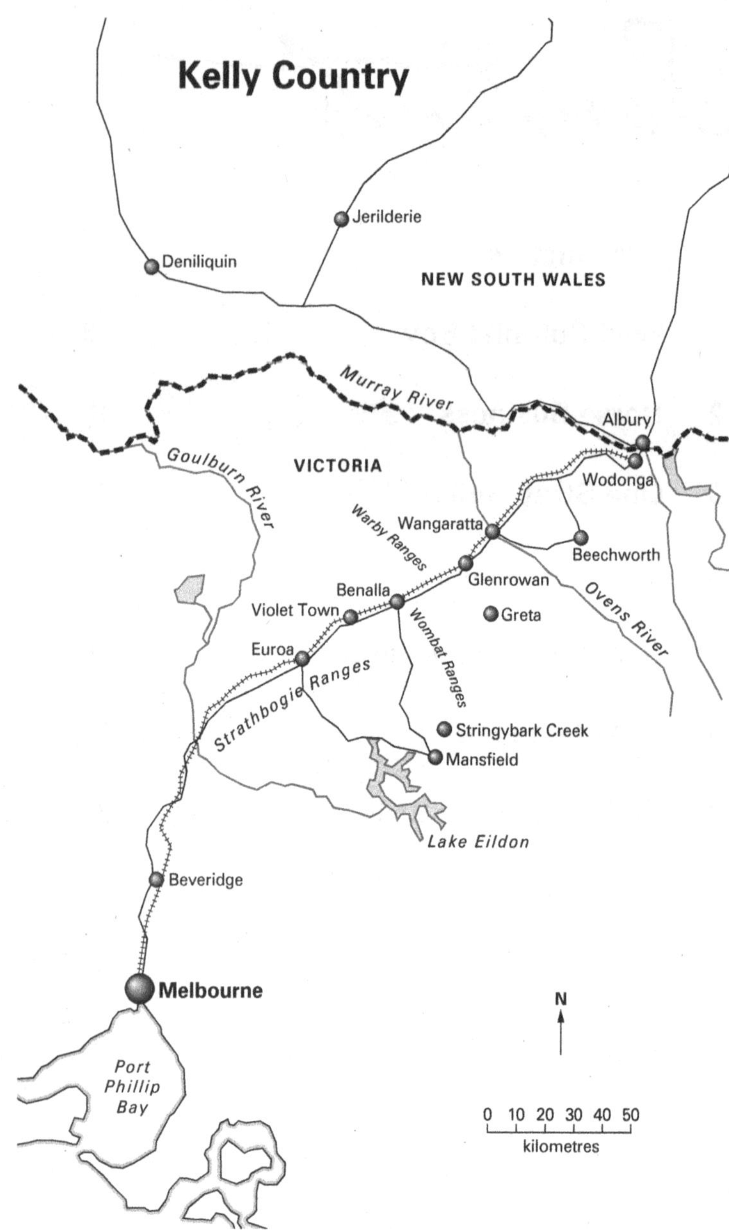
Kelly Country
Jerilderie
Deniliquin
NEW SOUTH WALES
Murray River
Albury
Wodonga
VICTORIA
Goulburn River
Warby Ranges
Wangaratta
Beechworth
Glenrowan
Ovens River
Benalla
Violet Town
Greta
Wombat Ranges
Euroa
Strathbogie Ranges
Stringybark Creek
Mansfield
Lake Eildon
Beveridge
Melbourne
Port Phillip Bay
N
0 10 20 30 40 50
kilometres

Introduction

Ned Kelly was a horse and cattle thief, a bank robber and a murderer. He was in trouble with the law from the age of 12. He spent three years in jail before he turned 20. By his own admission, he stole hundreds of horses and cattle. He robbed two banks. He killed three men.

When he was hanged in 1880, his story refused to be buried with him. Now, more than 100 years after his death, interest in the man and his story is as strong as it has ever been. Hundreds of books have been written about him. Films have been made. Famous artists have used Ned as a subject.

This fascination with Ned isn't a modern phenomenon. When he was sentenced to death, people rallied to save Ned's life. Alongside his family and legal representatives, thousands of ordinary people joined in the fight for his survival. A petition to reprieve him collected 32,000 signatures in just five days.

Why are we fascinated with this criminal? What is it about Ned Kelly that makes him so interesting? Why is he one of the most famous Australians of all time?

Photo from Ned's record sheet

Wild Colonial Boy

What if you were there...

The Irish are all the same. A bunch of brawling thieves. And don't tell me I've got no right to say that. I should know, I live among a great brood of them – the Kellys and their relations the Quinns and the Lloyds. I'm no squatter. I've worked hard all my life. I've paid for my land, all 250 acres of it, with the sweat off my brow. No one could call me rich, but compared to the Kelly clan I'm a wealthy man. They live in ramshackle huts, whole families in one room like herds of animals.

Old Mr Quinn's not a bad bloke, but his sons are a pack of louts. Nothing's safe. I have to keep my eyes on my few horses day and night, for fear of them disappearing. The women aren't much better than the men. You couldn't call them ladies. They scream abuse at you if you so much as look at them and they seem to marry fellows even worse than their brothers. I don't know what's to become of this colony if these are the sort of people who are allowed to settle. I'd rather have the convicts. Most of them have had the flashness knocked out of them by the time they're freed.

I thought Red Kelly might make something of himself, but he didn't. He turned to drink, God rest his soul. Now his wife and children are left to fend for themselves. The boys are always in trouble. If they're not stealing chickens, they're "borrowing" horses which they ride around, jumping fences and creeks. Sometimes the owners find the horses back in their paddocks a week or two later, exhausted and in need of being reshod. Sometimes they never see them again.

One of my horses went missing the week before last. A fine black mare with a flash on her head shaped like a diamond. I'd sent one of the farmhands over to the Quinns' and the Kellys' to scout around and see if he could find the horse, but there was no sign of her. I even told him to offer a reward for her return. But they were all playing dumb. I thought I'd seen the last of her.

Then the oldest of the Kelly boys came up to the house today. Ned, I think his name is. There he was with his hat pushed back on his head wearing a patched shirt and boots three sizes too big for him. He'd obviously just combed his hair for the visit. He has these dark penetrating eyes – I felt like he was seeing right into me, reading my thoughts. He was holding my mare.

"I found this horse wandering up in the Strathbogie Ranges," he said, those eyes now wide and innocent. "I thought she might be the one that you lost."

It was my horse all right. Even if she didn't have my brand on it, I would have recognised the white mark on her head anywhere. The lad was stroking the animal's head as he spoke. The horse, which is a nervous beast, was nuzzling his hand like she'd known him all her life. There was no way in the world that horse had been living wild in the bush for two weeks. It had been well fed and groomed as well. The lad had obviously stolen her. Sure enough. What did he say next?

"I'll be entitled to the reward then. What was it? Fifteen shillings?" Bold as brass even though he can't be any older than 12.

"You get outta my sight before I tan your hide," I told him.

I can't repeat the foul mouthful I got in return.

Still, the horse is in better condition than when it went missing. The boy obviously knows a bit about horses. Pity he can't put it to better use, but with his father gone and no one to guide him but his larrikin uncles, I can't see him making anything of himself.

Jacob Barker, selector

Early Days

Ned Kelly was born in 1854 in the bush not far north of Melbourne. His father was called Red because of his red hair. He was a freed Irish convict, who had served his seven-year sentence in the penal colony of Van Diemen's Land (present day Tasmania) for stealing two pigs. Ned's mother, Ellen, was also Irish. Her large family, the Quinns, had emigrated to Australia when she was just nine years old.

> **"Everyone looks on me like a black snake."**
> Letter to Sergeant Babington, July 1870

The Kellys were poor people, but Red made a little money in the goldfields and was able to buy 41 acres of land near the small town of Beveridge. The family grew, and for a while it looked like the Kellys were on their way to being successful farmers. This period of good fortune didn't last long. Ned's father had no experience as a farmer. The conditions in Victoria, from drought to flood, were unfamiliar to even experienced farmers. Beveridge didn't flourish as expected. The road to Sydney skirted around the town, instead of going through it and bringing more business. The Kelly land lost value. Before Ned's third birthday, his father got into debt and had to sell most of the land for half its original price. Things didn't improve.

Selectors versus Squatters

When Ned was 12 years old his father died. A widow with seven children could not afford to buy land, but Ned's mother was determined that the family would have land of their own. She didn't want them to be like poor tenant farmers in Ireland, under the thumb of some rich English landowner. The government had a way for poor people to buy land. It was called selection. A family would "select" a piece of land from allotments in unsettled areas and pay rent on it. If they paid their rent regularly for around seven years and looked after the land, doing what the government called "improvements", the land would become theirs. The improvements involved building homes and other farm buildings, clearing areas of bush to make fields and putting up fences.

"Whitty and Burns, not being satisfied with all the picked land on King River and Boggy Creek...paid heavy rent for all the open ground, so as a poor man could not keep his stock, and impounded every beast they could catch, even off Government roads."
Ned's complaints against squatters, Cameron Letter, December 1878

It was a hard life. To survive, the selectors grew wheat and vegetables and kept cattle. They had to produce enough to feed themselves and earn enough to pay rent and do the required improvements on the land. This could be achieved with a lot of hard work when the conditions were right, but that wasn't always the case. There were seasons when there was no rain and the crops died. There were bushfires that could destroy years of hard work in one afternoon. The government wanted the selectors to grow wheat, but often the land wasn't good to start off with and was unsuited to wheat growing.

The best land, vast areas of it, was owned by the squatters. Today we call someone who lives illegally in a house a squatter. At the beginning of white settlement in the 1800s, squatters were men who claimed thousands of hectares of rural land in New South Wales and then in Victoria. They legally took whatever land they wanted. Even though the rich squatters had the biggest and the best pieces of land, they were unhappy about the government allowing poor people to take up selections. If any cattle belonging to selectors wandered onto squatters' land, they impounded it and the selectors had to pay to get their own stock back. The selectors resented the squatters who had got the best land for nothing.

Head of the Family

Ned's mother selected a piece of land near the town of Greta on the Eleven Mile Creek. Ned had to work hard on his family's land, cutting down trees, digging out stumps, making fences. Ned wasn't the eldest child in the family, but he was the eldest son. After his father's death, he became the head of the family. As role models he had his uncles and cousins. If they taught Ned anything, it wasn't how to be an honest law-abiding citizen. A dozen of his relatives had criminal records. Between them they were arrested more than 60 times in Ned's lifetime. There was always one of Ned's relatives in jail for something.

Ned had his first brush with the police in 1867, just after his father died. A neighbour claimed Ned had stolen his horse and reported the theft to the police. Though it was noted in the *Police Gazette,* fortunately for Ned, the charge was dropped and nothing came of it.

Local Hero

Other local people suspected that Ned had stolen horses from them, including a family called the Sheltons. But Ned did something that made this family forget about their missing horse and remember Ned with gratitude. Their young son, Dick, was walking to school one day when he fell into the river. Eleven-year-old Ned happened to be passing by and jumped into the river to rescue the drowning lad.

The grateful Sheltons praised Ned's bravery and gave him a strange reward. It was a specially made green silk sash, seven feet long and trimmed with a fringe made of real gold threads. It was meant to be worn over one shoulder. Ned was very proud of his sash and wore it on special occasions.

Horseplay

As Ned grew up, he developed a love of horses. Dressed in moleskin pants and high leather boots, Ned found time between his farm chores to become an excellent horseman. He liked to show off his riding skills by riding down the main street of Greta on unbroken horses. The residents of Greta stood back in fear as the wild horses tried unsuccessfully to buck him off.

There was not much in the way of entertainment in small country towns in the 1870s. Community picnics and sports meetings were occasions that everyone looked forward to. People came from miles around to attend. At these events, Ned performed demonstrations of trick riding. On a galloping horse he would lean down out of his saddle to snatch up a handkerchief from the ground. He would also kneel on the horse's back as it leapt over fences at lightning speed.

Further Education

Ned went to school for less than two years. He must have been a bright boy because in that time he managed to learn how to read, write and do basic arithmetic. When Ned was ten, his father spent six months in jail for stealing a cow. Ned left school to take his father's place on the farm. That was the end of his schooling, but not the end of his education.

Four years later, Ned became an apprentice. Not as you might expect to a builder or a stockman, but to a bushranger. Harry Power wasn't a very impressive looking bushranger. He was short, middle-aged, bad-tempered and he had problems with his bowels. He wasn't very successful either. He had quite a talent for getting caught by the police. Harry spent 32 years in jail – almost half his life.

When Ned was born, Victoria had only been a colony separate from New South Wales for three years.

Juvenile Bushranger

The bushranger and his young assistant specialised in highway robbery. They would hide in the Strathbogie Ranges and suddenly appear on the road-side, pointing guns at unsuspecting travellers and demanding their money and valuables. They didn't earn a fortune, but £10 here, a gold watch there and the occasional good quality saddle made it worth their while.

Ned's mother didn't object to her son becoming a bushranger. She probably looked forward to getting Ned's cut of the spoils. Mrs Kelly made money illegally herself, by selling alcohol to passing travellers. Ned didn't like the life of a bushranger though. Sleeping outside in all kinds of weather, eating poorly and putting up with Harry's bad moods wasn't much fun. After just a few months as an apprentice bushranger, Ned left Harry and went back home. He had become known as Power's apprentice though and troopers arrived to arrest him early the next morning.

Ned had unusual eyes. A policeman once said that he had "dingo eyes". A doctor who tended to Ned said he had what was known as "Alexandrite" eyes. When people with Alexandrite eyes become angry or excited they glow red.

Young Ned spent several weeks in jail but was released without going to trial. Harry was caught after Ned's release, and believed that Ned had told the police where his hideout was. It wasn't Ned who got the £500 reward for Harry's capture though, it was one of Ned's uncles.

Out of Luck

Ned was lucky that neither of his early brushes with the law had led to him going to prison. But it wasn't long before he ended up in jail. He got caught up in an ugly argument between two hawkers (people who travelled around the countryside selling goods to farmers). They exchanged insults, and then punches. Ned was drawn into a fight that had nothing to do with him.

It wasn't a serious crime, but this time his luck ran out. Ned claimed he was innocent but he was charged with "violent assault". His sentence was to pay a fine of £10 plus an additional sum of £60 as a bond that he would not get into trouble again. This doesn't sound like a lot of money, but in 1869 £50 was as much as a labouring man would earn in a year. Ned's family managed to scrape together the £60, but couldn't find the other £10. Instead of paying the fine, Ned had to serve six months in jail. He was 15 years old.

Ned, aged 15, taken when he first went to prison.

Horse Business

What if you were there...

I was on my way to Greta yesterday driving my hawker's wagon. Young Ned Kelly rode up beside me looking very pleased with himself. He was astride a beautiful chestnut mare.

"I just had a bit of a holiday in Wangaratta," he told me, even though I didn't ask.

"That's a nice piece of horse flesh you've got there," I said.

"She's not mine," he said, regretfully patting the horse. "She belongs to a friend of my mother's."

"And what's this fine horse's name?" I asked.

"He didn't have a name for her, but I call her Lady. I'll be sorry to give her back. We cut quite a

flash in Wangaratta, Lady and me. There she was, strutting down the main street. When we did a bit of trick riding, it was like we'd been doing it for years. She was as gentle as a lamb when the publican's daughters rode her, but every now and then she'd shake her head and rear up a bit, just to give them a thrill."

The boy sighed. "Now it's back to splitting fence posts."

As we rode over the bridge into Greta, Constable Hall waved Ned over. Hall's a big, fat tub of lard with a fearful temper. Ned didn't seem to like him any more than I do. "Morning, Senior Constable," he said with a hint of sarcasm in his voice.

"Can you just come over to the station for a minute, Ned?" asked the constable cheerily. "There's a few more papers just arrived that you have to sign."

I pulled up outside the hotel. Ned gave me a long-suffering look and rode over to the police station. The lad's not long out of jail and still on a bond to keep the peace. He wouldn't want to upset the police. He was about to dismount when Hall grabbed hold of his jacket.

"I'm arresting you," Hall shouted, "for stealing this horse."

Ned pulled away from him. There was a rip as his jacket tore. The fat constable made another grab at Ned. Ned allowed himself to be pulled off the horse and the constable fell on his back in the dust with Ned on top of him. The mare reared up. As soon as her hooves hit the ground again, she started galloping away. Ned, caring more about the horse than the policeman, got up to run after her. He'd only taken two steps when Hall called out to him.

"Stop where you are," he shouted, "or I'll have the pleasure of shooting you dead."

Ned turned on his heels and found Hall's revolver in his face. Hall was sweating with the exertion of getting up so quickly. Ned was bristling with anger. After all, the lad had only just got out of jail and the pigs were already trying to lag him again.

"Shoot and be damned," Ned shouted.

Hall pulled the trigger. The gun was aimed right at Ned's head not four foot away. Even clumsy Hall couldn't miss from that distance. I was only a few feet away myself. I heard the crack as the gun fired, saw a plume of smoke rising. Ned didn't move a muscle. No doubt he thought he'd seen his last. But the gun had misfired. Ned was frozen to the spot. Hall moved towards him. He pulled the trigger again – and again. The gun misfired for a second and then a third time.

Ned suddenly came to life. There were still three shots left in the gun. It was pure luck that he'd survived so far. He wasn't ready to trust to luck any more. He leapt at Hall, one hand grabbing the revolver, the other getting a fistful of the constable's fat neck. Hall squawked like a chicken about to have its neck wrung. Before I knew it, there were half a dozen men on Ned's back. Hall pulled the revolver from Ned's grasp and bashed him over the head with it again and again. I went over to try and stop him, before he killed the boy. Blood was pouring from his head, but Ned was staring straight at Hall's sweating face. His eyes flickered. He was holding on to consciousness by sheer force of will. I'd guess he didn't want to give that fat pig the satisfaction of saying he'd knocked Ned Kelly out cold.

James Gloster, hawker

Short and Sweet

Ned had to have nine stitches in his head. He had only been released from jail a few weeks and he was in trouble again. This time it was more serious. Ned thought the horse he was riding belonged to a man called "Wild" Wright who had been staying at the Kelly house. The horse had been put in a paddock, but had got out and disappeared into the bush. The horse was found after Wild had left. There was one important fact that Wild hadn't mentioned to the Kellys – the horse wasn't his. He had stolen it.

Ned had made an enemy of Senior Constable Hall the previous year. Hall had asked Ned to draw his uncle Jimmy Quinn into a fight so that the police could arrest him. Uncle Jimmy was a troublemaker. Ned didn't like him. He agreed to help Constable Hall. He had no trouble annoying his uncle enough to make him pick a fight. He ran to the police station for protection and Hall arrested Uncle Jimmy. But when Ned had to tell his story in front of a judge and jury, he confessed that Hall had put him up to it. Since then, Hall had been out to get Ned. When Ned rode into town on a stolen horse, Hall had his opportunity.

On Ned's prison record, under "Particular Marks" is a list of nine scars. Four of them were on his head and were probably the result of Constable Hall hitting him with the butt of his revolver.

If Constable Hall's gun had worked properly, the story of Ned Kelly would have ended right there and no one would have remembered his name.

Justice

Ned insisted that he didn't know the horse was stolen. If he had known, he would hardly have been so stupid as to ride it around Wangaratta in broad daylight. Constable Hall was keen to get Ned back for letting him down in court. The judge was happy to make an example of the young larrikin. There was a problem though. The horse had been reported stolen while Ned was still in jail, so he couldn't be charged with horse stealing. He was charged instead with receiving a stolen horse. Wild Wright, the man who had actually stolen the horse, was sentenced to 18 months in jail. Ned was sentenced to three years hard labour.

"I threw big cowardly Hall on his belly I straddled him and rooted both spurs onto his thighs he roared like a big calf attacked by dogs."
Ned's version of his arrest by Hall, Jerilderie Letter, February 1879

Breaking Rocks

Prison life was hard. First Ned had to serve three months of solitary confinement – one month for each year of his sentence. This was the prison policy at the

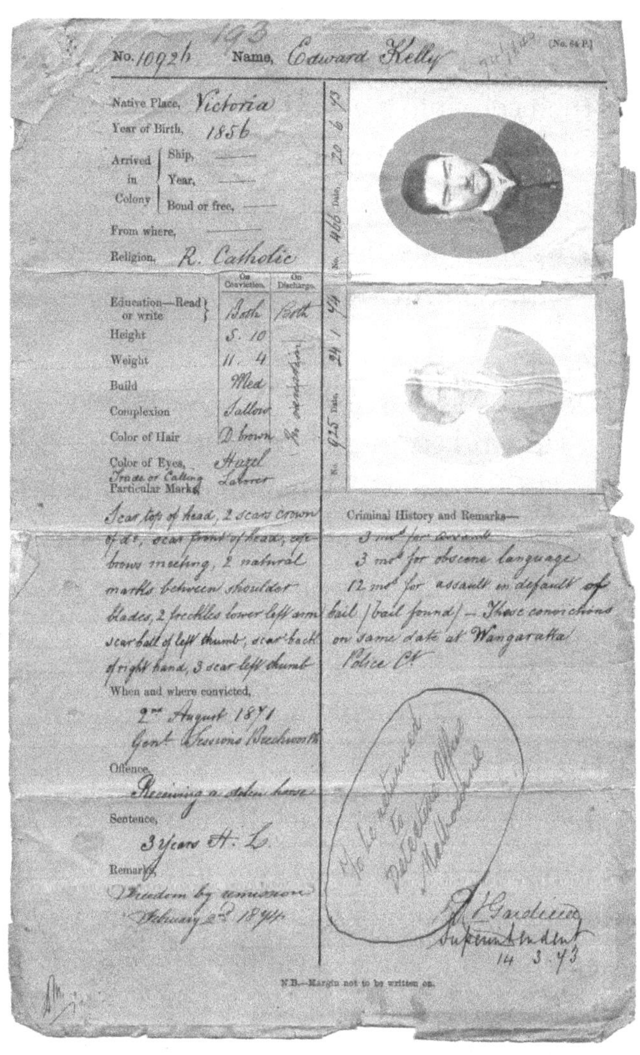

No. 10926 Name, Edward Kelly [No. 84 P.]

Native Place, Victoria

Year of Birth, 1856

Arrived in Colony: Ship, —— Year, —— Bond or free, ——

From where, ——

Religion, R. Catholic

No. 466 Date. 20 6 73

No. 925 Date. 24 1 79

	On Conviction.	On Discharge.
Education—Read or write	Both	Both
Height	5. 10	
Weight	11. 4	
Build	Med	
Complexion	Sallow	
Color of Hair	D. brown	
Color of Eyes,	Hazel	
Trade or Calling	Labourer	

Particular Marks

Scar top of head, 2 scars crown of do, scar front of head, eye-brows meeting, 2 natural marks between shoulder blades, 2 freckles lower left arm scar ball of left thumb, scar back of right hand, 3 scar left thumb

When and where convicted,

2nd August 1871
Genl Sessions Beechworth

Offence,

Receiving a stolen horse

Sentence,

3 years H. L.

Remarks,

Freedom by remission
February 2nd 1874

Criminal History and Remarks—

3 mos for assault
3 mos for obscene language
12 mos for assault in default of bail (bail found) — These convictions on same date at Wangaratta Police Ct

To be returned to Detective Office Melbourne

Superintendent
14 3 73

N.B.—Margin not to be written on.

Ned's prison record listing his "particular marks", including scars and freckles.

time. Locked in a cell by himself, he was not permitted to speak to anyone. Ned and other prisoners serving similar sentences were allowed out of their cells into the yard for one hour of exercise each day. So that the isolation continued even when the prisoners were together for this short time, they had to wear hoods that completely covered their heads, with only two small holes for them to see through.

The rest of Ned's sentence was served doing hard labour. He worked in government quarries cutting blocks of bluestone with a hammer and chisel. Then he joined work gangs and helped build sea walls around Port Phillip Bay. Six months were taken off Ned's sentence for good behaviour. He was 19 when he was released.

Home Free

He arrived home in February 1874 to find his world had changed. One of his sisters was dead; another was married. His brother Jim was serving a five-year jail sentence for cattle stealing. His mother was about to remarry, and he had a new baby half-sister.

Fresh from two-and-a-half years in prison, Ned was determined never to go back there again. He got a job in a timber mill. He wanted to get his revenge

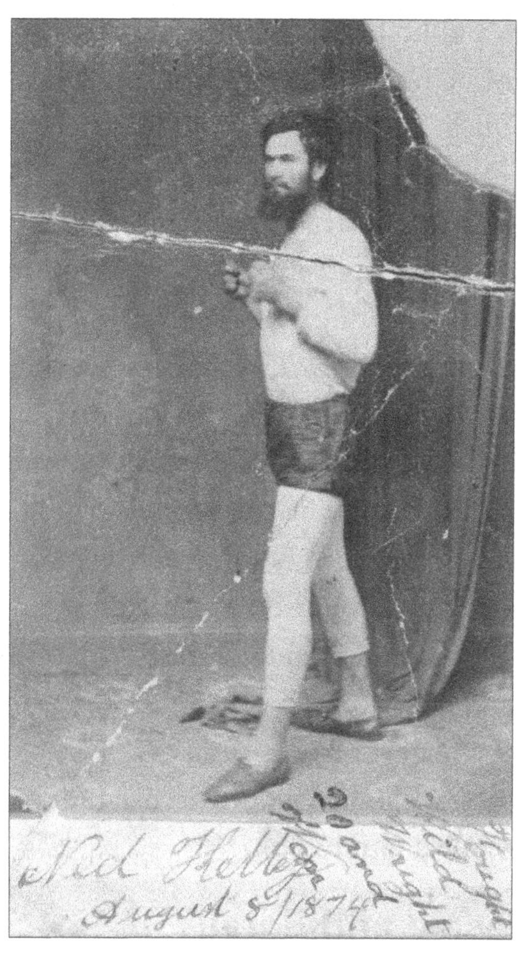

Ned after beating Wild Wright in a boxing match.

on Wild Wright who had been the cause of his imprisonment, but he didn't want to get into trouble again. A public brawl could have easily ended up with him being arrested, so instead Ned agreed to fight Wild in an organised boxing match. Wild was an experienced fighter, but the years of hard work in prison and months of tree felling since his release meant that Ned was a strong young man. He had the satisfaction of beating Wild Wright.

He spent the next three years working hard, earning an honest living. He had jobs driving bullock teams, breaking horses and shearing, but most of the work he did was felling trees for a sawmill. He was a trusted worker and became an overseer, yet the period of honest toil didn't last. Ned later claimed that he had been driven to crime by what we would today call police persecution and harassment. He said that whenever a horse or a cow went missing in the district, the police would accuse him or another member of his family.

Wholesale and Retail

By the beginning of 1877, Ned had given up tree felling and bullock driving. He had passed up the chance of continuing to work for his sawmill bosses. Instead, he had taken up what he called "wholesale and retail horse and cattle dealing". This was Ned's idea of a joke. He really meant horse and cattle theft.

He was joined in this venture by his brother Dan; his step-father, George King; some of his cousins and two friends called Aaron Sherritt and Joe Byrne.

This gang of thieves was no ragtag band. The operation was well organised. The gang found an old hut, deep in the Wombat Ranges. They fixed up the hut and cleared many acres around it. They built fences. They took the stolen stock up to this remote spot where they could corral them away from the prying eyes of settlers, squatters and policemen.

"I was blamed for stealing this bull from James Whitty... I was blamed for stealing a mob of calves from Whitty and Farrell which I knew nothing about. I began to think they wanted me to give them something to talk about. Therefore I started wholesale and retail horse and cattle dealing."

Ned's reason for turning to horse theft, Jerilderie Letter

Tricks of the Trade

Stealing the stock was easy enough. The tricky thing was to sell the animals again without the buyer realising they were stolen. One way to do this was to change the brand. Every stock owner had his own brand – a symbol, such as initials, that was burnt into the hide of the animal. This way, if an animal got lost or stolen, the owner could prove it was his. The gang devised ways of changing brands, for instance by turning an H into an HP joined together. As a fresh brand would have looked suspicious, they found ways of making new brands look old. One technique they used was to pull out the animal's hairs with tweezers in the shape of the new brand, then prick the bare skin with a needle that had been dipped in iodine. This made the skin burn and the mark it left looked like an old brand.

In the 1800s, policemen were known as "troopers" or "the traps". The word "troop" comes from the Latin word "troppus" which means a "flock". Troop is a collective word for soldiers. Troopers were members of a troop, especially of cavalry soldiers. In Australia, the word was also used to describe a mounted policeman.
A "trap" was a person, usually a policeman, whose job it was to catch or "trap" criminals. This word continued to be used in Australia long after it had disappeared from usage in England.

The gang stole stock in Victoria and then took the animals over the Murray River, swimming them across at deserted places instead of using busy bridges. They then sold the animals openly in saleyards in New South Wales, far from their owners and reports of their theft.

Sometimes one of the gang would pretend he was a squatter's son taking horses to sell at a market. He would stop at another squatter's property and ask if he could put his animals in a paddock overnight so they didn't stray. Another gang member would arrive and say he was interested in buying the horses. The two would agree on a price and then ask the squatter to witness the receipt that they wrote out. They would then pretend to go off in opposite directions. This way there was a "genuine" receipt to offer as proof that the animals weren't stolen when they really tried to sell them.

Close of Business

The gang weren't the only ones involved in horse and cattle theft at the time. There was a complicated network of thieves. Thieves stole from other thieves and it was impossible to tell whether stock offered for sale was genuine or not. Buying stolen stock was considered to be almost as serious a crime as stealing it.

Eventually, other men were arrested for receiving horses that the gang had stolen, though Ned was suspected of being the main culprit. Knowing that it was only a matter of time until someone informed on him, Ned sold his remaining horses and disappeared into the bush.

Ned's brother Dan decided to go home. With no evidence to prove that he was involved in the theft of stock, the police left him alone – for a while. Before long, though, a warrant was issued for Dan's arrest. He was charged with a theft that had happened more than six months earlier.

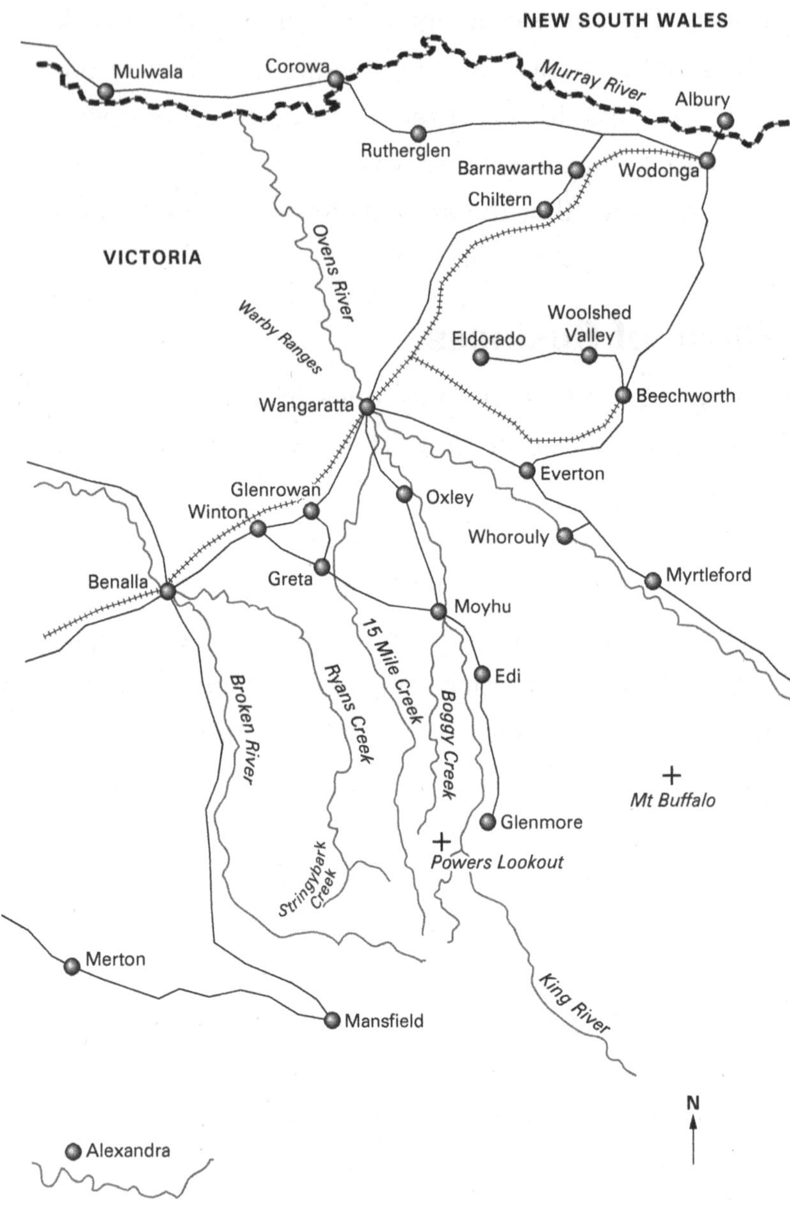
NEW SOUTH WALES
Mulwala
Corowa
Murray River
Albury
Rutherglen
Barnawartha
Wodonga
Chiltern
VICTORIA
Ovens River
Warby Ranges
Woolshed Valley
Eldorado
Beechworth
Wangaratta
Everton
Glenrowan
Winton
Oxley
Whorouly
Myrtleford
Benalla
Greta
Moyhu
Edi
Broken River
Ryans Creek
15 Mile Creek
Boggy Creek
Mt Buffalo
Glenmore
Powers Lookout
Stringybark Creek
King River
Merton
Mansfield
N
Alexandra

One Stray Bullet

What if you were there...

The day had seemed no different to any other. Mother and I had spent it washing the sheets and making quince jam. We had just eaten our dinner. I was rocking the baby, looking down at her innocent sleeping face, thinking here's another mouth to feed, but also another sister. Funny how a new baby can appear in the family, a stranger, unable to speak or do anything but cry, but within two days you can't help but love them fiercely. My mother was heaping coals on the fire around the bread she was baking. The yeasty smell was starting to overpower the smell of smoke. My brother Daniel had come in late and was still eating.

There was a knock at the door. I waited for Daniel to get up and answer it, but he made no move, concentrating on demolishing the plate of stew in front of him. I sighed and gently lowered the baby into her cradle – actually a fruit box on roughly cut rockers. Another more insistent knock and Danny finally hauled himself up and over to the door, still holding his knife and fork and yelling, "Can't a man eat in peace?"

Dan opened the door. "I've come to arrest you, Dan Kelly, on a charge of horse stealing." I recognised our visitor's voice. It was Constable Fitzpatrick from Benalla. I'd met him before at the Sports Day. I'd thought him quite handsome at the time.

Danny glanced back at mother and me. "Can I at least finish my dinner?" he said. No one invited him in, but Fitzpatrick came in anyway. He didn't bother to take off his helmet.

Mother turned to the trooper, her hands on her hips, her face red from the fire. "Where's the warrant, then?" she demanded. She turned to Dan. "You shouldn't have let him in if he's got no warrant."

"It's all right, Mother," Danny said calmly,

sitting down at the table again and scraping up the last of his stew. "Is that bread ready yet?"

Mother pulled the loaf of bread from the fire and put it on the table. Danny wasn't in a hurry. He hacked an inch-thick slice from one end and used it to mop up his gravy. He drained his tin mug of tea. Finally he pushed his chair away from the table. "I'll just get my coat."

Danny went into the other room. Mother followed him, still protesting that he didn't have to go anywhere if there was no warrant. Constable Fitzpatrick came over to where I was sitting with the baby. He leaned his sweaty face towards me. I smelt the brandy on his breath and the stale smell of a shirt needing a good wash.

"Don't you dare touch me." I pushed him away. Fitzpatrick staggered back onto a chair. He reached out and grabbed me by the arm and pulled me onto his lap. "Get your greasy hands off me," I yelled.

Danny and mother rushed back into the room. I was thrown to the floor as Fitzpatrick stood up. Mother, screaming abuse at the policeman, picked up the coal shovel and brought it crashing down on his helmet while he was still fumbling to get his revolver out of its holster. Danny dived at the gun. At that moment the door was flung open and Ned was standing in the doorway. There was a flash and a crack as a gun went off. Fitzpatrick screamed out like a girl. The revolver had gone off as Dan grappled to take it from Fitzpatrick. A bullet had nicked the trooper's wrist. My brothers were on their knees holding him down. They both had guns held at his head.

"If you touch my sister again," said Ned, his voice trembling with rage. "There'll be a bullet in your head next time."

Kate Kelly, Ned's sister

The Whole Truth

This isn't quite the version of events that Constable Alexander Fitzpatrick reported to his colleague in Benalla when he woke him at 2 a.m. with his wrist bandaged and his helmet dented out of shape. He said Mrs Kelly attacked him with the shovel, unprovoked, and then Ned appeared and shot him in the arm. He said that Ned dug the bullet from his wrist and bandaged it up, apologising for shooting at him. Ned then begged him not to let on that it was Ned who'd fired the shot. Fitzpatrick didn't mention Kate.

> **"The police got great credit and praise in the papers for arresting the mother of 12 children one an infant on her breast and those two quiet hard working innocent men who would not know the difference [between] a revolver and a saucepan handle and kept them six months awaiting trial and then convicted them on the evidence of the meanest article that ever the sun shone on."**
> Ned's view of the police, Fitzpatrick in particular, Jerilderie Letter

Seven versions of these events have been recorded.

Lapses of Memory

In Ned's version of the story, he was more than 600 kilometres away at the time, still keeping a low profile. He said he heard about the incident later from his family. They told him that Fitzpatrick pulled his revolver and threatened to blow his mother's brains out. Dan disarmed the policeman

Constable Fitzpatrick in police uniform.

before he could carry out his threat and no shots were fired.

Mrs Kelly claimed that Fitzpatrick tried to kiss 14-year-old Kate and "the boys" were defending her honour.

Kate was reported as saying that she was alone when Fitzpatrick came to the house. Her brothers arrived just in time to witness Fitzpatrick "behaving improperly" to her.

"I have heard from a trooper that he never knew Fitzpatrick to be one night sober and that he sold his sister to a chinaman...the deceit and cowardice is too plain to be seen in the puny cabbage hearted looking face."

More on Fitzpatrick, Jerilderie Letter

A neighbour, Brickey Williamson, claimed he stood between Mrs Kelly and Fitzpatrick and took the shovel from her before she had a chance to hit the policeman.

Ned's brother Jim said he was told that Fitzpatrick shot himself accidentally during the scuffle with Dan.

Ned's cousin Tom Lloyd said Fitzpatrick was about to shoot Ned when Dan grappled him to the floor. The constable accidentally shot himself in the scuffle. He cut his wrist on the door latch.

We will never know what really happened, but the incident had far-reaching effects. Even though it only lasted a few minutes, the confrontation with Fitzpatrick was, ultimately, what turned the Kelly brothers from horse thieves into hunted outlaws.

Bush Telegraph

Though Ned claimed he wasn't at the house on that fateful day in April 1878, it seems likely that he was. Though he said no shots were fired, the evidence suggests that they were. But whatever the exact sequence of events was, the result was the same – Ned and Dan knew they were in trouble with the police and they both made themselves scarce. What they didn't know, what they didn't imagine in their wildest dreams, was that they weren't the only ones in trouble. The Kelly brothers rode off that same night to hide deep in the bush. It was some time before they heard the news. The following day, their mother, a brother-in-law and Brickey Williamson had all been arrested for the attempted murder of Constable Fitzpatrick.

Alexander Fitzpatrick was only a young man himself. Younger than Ned, he was just 21 years old at the time of the "Fitzpatrick Affair". Fitzpatrick was thrown out of the police force three years later. Throughout his life he continued to deny that he had molested Kate Kelly, but he went down in history as the man who caused the Kelly Outbreak.

It must have been a terrible shock for Ned when he heard this news. He had high-tailed it from the scene of the crime and his own mother, with a three-day-old baby, had been arrested instead. His mother had been guilty only of hitting a man with a shovel. The two men were completely innocent. Brickey was guilty of nothing more than being present at the house when the shooting took place. Bill Skilling, who was married to Ned's sister Maggie, hadn't even been there at the time. Fitzpatrick swore that Bill was present, though it seems more likely that the other man was actually Ned's friend Joe Byrne, and that Fitzpatrick made a mistake.

Adding to Ned's worries, no one had yet come forward to pay the £200 bail, so his mother and newborn sister were in a freezing jail with winter setting in.

Enterprise

The Kelly brothers didn't go far. They hid in the Wombat Ranges, close enough to home to hear regular news from friends who rode out to bring them food and other supplies. On hearing about his mother's arrest, Ned immediately swung into action. He and Dan set up in an abandoned hut. Ned wanted to raise money for the legal defence of Mrs Kelly and the others. The two Kelly boys set about panning for gold at abandoned gold mines. They built a still and planted crops to provide the ingredients needed to brew whisky. Ned's plan was that they would then sell the gold and the whisky to get money for a lawyer.

Guilty as Charged

Two months later, Ned was relieved to hear that someone had finally come forward to pay Mrs Kelly's bail money. She was able to return home until the trial. It was a long six months before the trial.

The next news Ned heard was not so good. Sir Redmond Barry was to be the presiding judge at the trial. His determination to wipe out crime in the Victorian countryside was well known. There was worse news to come. All three were found guilty. Mrs Kelly was sentenced to three years hard labour. Skilling and Williamson each received sentenced of six years hard labour. These were very severe sentences. Justice Barry said he hoped that his tough sentencing would be a lesson to the gang of lawless people who were operating around the Greta district. He believed it would result in Ned and his friends giving up their lawless ways.

Even though Ned's mother remarried in 1874 and became Ellen King, everybody including Ned, the police and the newspapers still referred to her as Mrs Kelly.

The Kelly Gang Is Born

Justice Barry couldn't have been more wrong. His action of sentencing Mrs Kelly so severely only made her sons more convinced of the injustice of the legal system. Yet Ned and Dan's time as wanted criminals might have ended there. Through an uncle, Ned made an offer to surrender if his mother was freed. The offer was not taken up. A reward of £100 was offered for information resulting in the capture of each of the Kelly boys.

Steve Hart, a good friend of Dan's, had finished his prison sentence for illegally using a horse just after the Kelly brothers went into hiding. He had learned nothing from the experience. Instead of taking up honest work alongside his father at the Hart family's property, he chose to join the Kellys. Joe Byrne, perhaps afraid that he would eventually be identified as the other man present at the Fitzpatrick incident, also joined the boys in the Wombat Ranges. The Kelly Gang was now complete.

Unreliable Witness

Fitzpatrick's position in the police force was shaky. He was not a good policeman. He was known to be unreliable and to drink too much. He may have thought that if he arrested Dan his superiors would be impressed by his efficiency and he would keep his job. Perhaps that was why he went out to arrest Dan before he had a warrant. Things didn't go as he planned.

Dan Kelly

Dan was only 17 when he became a fugitive with his elder brother. Like a modern teenager he was concerned about the way he looked and dressed. He and his gang (known as the Greta Mob) had their own particular style of dress. Dan liked to grow his hair long and wear his hat tilted at an angle. He also devised the strange fashion of wearing his hat strap under his nose instead of under his chin. People also said that he and his friends wore brightly coloured sashes around their waists when out riding. The two surviving photos of Dan were taken when he was about 16. They show a shy, good-looking boy who wouldn't look at the camera. He was dressed in rough, oversized, homemade-looking clothes and he had an air of self-consciousness.

Joe Byrne

Joe was Ned's best friend. In his youth he was not as "flash" as the Kelly boys and was remembered as being quiet and well-mannered. He was better educated than the Kellys. Joe had neat handwriting, his spelling was good and he also liked to read. Ned would later rely on him to help write his famous letters. It was also reported that he could speak Chinese. This came about because he was an opium addict and had constant dealings with the Chinese gold miners living in the Chinese camp at Beechworth. He was not wanted by the police and chose to be an outlaw.

Steve Hart

Dan's friend Steve was another volunteer outlaw. Although he had just served a year in jail for horse theft, he did not have the long association with crime and police attention that the Kellys did. He was a good horseman who rode horses at the local horse races and was remembered for jumping his horse over the railway gates. He was also a member of Dan's Greta Mob and it seems he was attracted by the idea of being a fugitive on the run from the police. No doubt he thought it sounded like a more exciting life than splitting fence posts.

Enemies of Society

What if you were there...

"Mother, I can't get to sleep. I keep having scary dreams. Mother, I'm frightened."

Why won't she come? I've been shouting out for a long time. The doctor gave her medicine out of his black bag. It stopped her crying, but now she can't hear me. "Please come, Mother."

I wish Mary or Laurie were awake. I can hear them breathing. How can they sleep? It's so dark. There's no moon. I can't see anything but a sprinkle of stars through the window. What's that noise? There's something outside my window. My heart's beating like a drum. Is it one of the Kellys come to get me?

I wish Father were here. I wouldn't be scared if he was here to protect us. My father's a trooper. He's got a jacket with gold on the sleeves and he wears a helmet like a big black egg squashed on his head. Some evenings when he comes home, he takes off his helmet and puts it on me. It's miles too big and comes down over my eyes. That always made him laugh. He won't be laughing anymore though. Last night he didn't come home. My father's dead. Ned Kelly did it. He shot him.

Father had been gone for a couple of days, searching for the Kelly Gang. They were wanted for trying to kill Constable Fitzpatrick. My father said we couldn't have that. He didn't think much of Constable Fitzpatrick, but he said people had to respect the troopers. The troopers are the law. If they don't respect them, they don't respect the law and if that's the case, no one's safe. He went off on Monday morning and he never came back.

I knew something was wrong when someone knocked on the front door. No one ever knocks on the front door. People who come to visit just walk round the back and sing out. It was another trooper. Mother made me go out into the garden.

I wasn't supposed to hear, but I crept round and sat under the window. I heard everything.

"I'm sorry to be the one to tell you this, Mrs Kennedy," he said. "But your husband is dead. He was killed in the line of duty."

Ned Kelly killed my father. He shot him in the chest. He killed two other troopers too. Only one got away. That was Constable McIntyre. He found a wombat hole and hid in it all night. He was too scared to come out in case the Kellys were looking for him. My father was only doing his job. All he was trying to do was bring in the Kellys so that they could go to court. That's a place where you go to find out if you're guilty or not. If they were guilty of trying to kill Constable Fitzpatrick, they'd go to jail. If they weren't guilty, then they'd be set free. That seems fair enough to me. It's not fair that someone can be shot just for doing their job.

Who's going to look after Mary and Laurie and me now? Who's going to go out and earn the money for food? Mary's the eldest and she's only nine. She could probably do some washing or mind a lady's babies. I don't think she'd earn enough to feed us all, though.

Laurie says that when he grows up he's going to be a trooper just like father. And if Ned Kelly is still alive then, he'll track him down and shoot him. Laurie says I'm not allowed to tell anybody – not even mother. If the Kellys find out, they'll come to the house and shoot him first.

What was that? There's something out there, I'm sure there is. Something made the stars disappear. It could have been a cloud or it might have been one of the Kelly Gang.

"Mother, can I come and sleep in your bed? Mother!"

Rose Kennedy, seven years old.

Target Practice

The Kelly Gang had been hiding out in the Wombat Ranges for six months, keeping themselves busy panning for gold and distilling whisky. They also spent a lot of time practising shooting. The trees around their hidden hut were marked with targets and there was evidence that they had been shot at, with increasing accuracy, many times. Ammunition was in short supply, so the bullets had all been dug out of the trees, melted down and made into new bullets.

The sawn-off shotgun used by Ned Kelly at Stringybark Creek was given to the Melbourne Museum of Applied Science. In the 1950s, someone decided it wasn't worth keeping and threw it out.

Some time after Mrs Kelly's trial, the gang heard news that the police had started a campaign to capture them. There were at least two groups of police out in the trackless hills in search of them, maybe three. It was only a matter of time before the police stumbled upon their camp.

Search Party

One group of four policemen left the town of Mansfield with enough supplies to enable them to search for a week. On the first day out they set up camp on the banks of Stringybark Creek. Little did they know that they were less than two kilometres from the Kellys' hideout. Constable McIntyre was given the job of cooking for the party. He thought it would be a good idea to shoot some parrots or perhaps a kangaroo so that the men could have fresh meat for their dinner.

In 1878, the telephone had only just been invented and wouldn't be in general use for a number of years. People communicated over long distance by telegraph, using morse code. The telegraph offices were closed over the weekend. Therefore when there was urgent news to send, it couldn't be sent until the telegraph offices opened on Monday morning.

The gang had been alone in the hills for months. Suddenly there was the sound of gunfire ringing out around the valleys. If the police were out in force looking for them, Ned decided they needed more guns and horses. Instead of waiting for the troopers to find them, they would go out after the troopers.

The Hunters Hunted

It wasn't hard to find the police camp. The gunshots had told the gang in which direction it lay and a huge campfire led them straight to it like a beacon. There were two policemen at the camp. They weren't on guard, looking out for the gang. One was cooking dinner. The other was tending the horses.

Ned and his mates were not well armed. Finding only two policemen was a stroke of luck. Ned emerged from the undergrowth and told the policemen to "Bail up". The others came out of hiding as well, to show the policemen that they were outnumbered. McIntyre raised his hands in surrender. The other policeman, Constable Lonigan, turned and dived for the cover of a nearby log, reaching for his revolver as he did. Ned fired. Lonigan was shot.

McIntyre stared in horror at his dead colleague. Ned questioned him while the others searched the camp. They discovered that there were two other policemen in the search party. It was late afternoon and they were due back at any moment. The Kelly Gang just had time to eat some of the food that Constable McIntyre had prepared before the other two policemen, Scanlon and Kennedy, returned.

Death at Stringybark Creek

McIntyre yelled out to his two colleagues that they were surrounded and they should give up their weapons. At first they didn't take him seriously and kept riding into the camp. Then Ned came out of hiding, followed by the other three gang members, now all properly armed with police guns. The two troopers didn't surrender though. Scanlon shot at Ned but narrowly missed him, the bullet singeing his beard. Ned shot back. He didn't miss. Scanlon

Men at the site of the Stringybark Creek shoot-out a week after the event.

fell from his horse. Sergeant Kennedy jumped down from his horse and, using the animal as a shield, shot at the outlaws. One of his bullets grazed Dan's shoulder. A second shot from Ned killed Scanlon.

The horses were frightened by the gunfire and in the commotion, McIntyre leapt onto Kennedy's rearing horse, which galloped off. At the same time, Kennedy ran into the bush for cover. Ned went after him. He followed Kennedy for some time until the policeman came out from cover and shot at Ned. Kennedy missed. Ned, his aim sure after months of target practice, shot Kennedy in the armpit. The wounded policeman turned and Ned shot him again.

Things had not turned out the way Ned had

planned. The gang had only wanted to take the policemen's weapons. The shaken bushrangers took the dead troopers' guns and searched the bodies for money and valuables.

Escape

Meanwhile, McIntyre was still clinging to Kennedy's horse as it galloped through the bush away from the scene of the gunfight. McIntyre had no control over the panicked animal and eventually a tree branch hit him and knocked him from the horse's back. McIntyre was terrified. At least two of his colleagues had been shot by ruthless bushrangers who, for all he knew, were right behind him with their guns aimed at him as well. As night fell, McIntyre scrambled into a wombat hole.

The police were so ill-equipped that when the police party left Mansfield to search for the bodies of Scanlon, Kennedy and Lonigan, they had to borrow guns from the townspeople.

The next morning, once he was sure there were no bushrangers around, McIntyre headed for home. He took off his boots so that he didn't leave any footprints. He walked barefoot towards the town of Mansfield. It was three in the afternoon before he reached the nearest farm.

Constable McIntyre didn't have much of a chance to rest after his ordeal. That same evening he led a party of police back to the camp to find the bodies of their colleagues.

Three Dead

Once again there were different reports of what happened at Stringybark Creek. McIntyre swore that Ned shot Lonigan as he was ducking for cover. Ned said that he didn't shoot him until he had taken cover behind a log, and he raised his head to shoot him. Ned admitted that he had shot Kennedy as he tried to surrender. He had thought he was turning to shoot him with his revolver. When Ned knelt at the side of the dying policeman, he saw that he had been mistaken. What he thought was a revolver in his hand was in fact a clot of blood which had run down his arm from his first wound. Ned said he shot Kennedy again as an act of mercy because the dying man was in so much pain. McIntyre said Ned shot a wounded man who was pleading for his life.

"We thought our country was woven with police, and we might have a chance of fighting them if we had firearms."
Ned's reason for attacking the police, Cameron Letter

"I called on them to throw up their hands. Scanlon slewed his horse round to gallop away, but turned again, and as quick as thought, fired at me with the rifle, and was in the act of firing again when I shot him."
Ned's version of the gunfight at Stringybark Creek, Cameron Letter

Whatever the circumstances, the result was the same. Three policemen were dead. Two women were widows. Nine children were fatherless. Ned had previously been wanted for the attempted killing of Fitzpatrick and horse theft. Now he was wanted for murder.

> **"This cannot be called wilful murder, for I was compelled to shoot them in my own defence, or lie down like a cur and die."**
> Ned defends his actions, Cameron Letter

Outlawed

Early the next morning, the Kelly Gang left the place where they had been hiding for the last six months. They probably thought that McIntyre had already raised the alarm and search parties would be out in force, but that wasn't the case. It wasn't until Monday morning that word reached Melbourne and plans for a major manhunt got under way.

Once the police authorities heard of the deaths, things started to move faster. In three weeks a special act of parliament had been hurriedly passed. Known as the Felons Apprehension Act, it declared that Ned Kelly, Dan Kelly and two other men whose names weren't known were outlaws and that anyone who came across them was entitled to kill them without question. The reward for their capture –

dead or alive – had been raised to £2000 – £500 for each outlaw.

If Ned had thought that killing the police search party would ease their situation, he had been wrong. Before, two parties of police had been after them – no more than eight men. Now the entire police force of Victoria was after them with a vengeance and any ordinary citizen could shoot them on sight.

Blunderers, Fools and Cowards

What if you were there...

This is my chance to become a hero. I'll be remembered as one of the men who captured Ned Kelly. At least, I hope so. We haven't captured him yet. I'm not sure who's supposed to be in charge here, Superintendent Nicolson or Superintendent Sadleir. I don't think they know either. If we caught the gang, I bet they'd both be shouting that they'd masterminded the whole thing. As we haven't caught sight of any outlaws yet, they're both hanging back and trying to get the other one to make all the decisions.

Superintendent Sadleir brought two native trackers with him. I've heard it said that they can track a rabbit in pouring rain and a fog. I don't doubt it. This morning they said they could see horse tracks. I thought they were making it up. I couldn't see anything more than the natural patterns of the earth. We followed them for three hours. I was sure that we were being led on a wild goose chase. Then an hour-and-a-half later they got very excited. They were jabbering away to each other in their strange native language, so none of us had the least idea what they were talking about. Then the old tracker, Doctor, they call him, said to Mr Sadleir that they'd found fresher tracks.

They were fresh enough that even I could see them. I couldn't tell how many horses, but it could easily have been four. We followed them for over an hour over some open country. Even when we crossed a rocky outcrop the trackers didn't lose the trail for a minute. The tracks led into some dense scrub. I could see the hoof prints disappearing into the trees. The trackers stopped dead and started jabbering to each other again. Then they suddenly turned away from the scrub and headed off down a slope to the east.

"Where are they going?" I shouted out, though it wasn't my place to say anything. "The trail

leads into the scrub. They're following a different set of tracks."

The natives tried to pretend they couldn't understand me, though they both looked sheepish.

Superintendent Nicolson looked at the thick scrub nervously. "These men know what they're doing," he said. "We're in their hands."

I stared into the scrub myself. The gums and tea-tree were dense and it was impossible to see more than a few feet into it, but I had a definite feeling that I was being watched. It made the hairs on the back of my neck stand on end. The Kellys were hiding in that scrub, I was certain. I tried to protest and got threatened with reduced pay if I didn't mind my own business. I reluctantly followed the search party.

We came to a billabong. The trackers began shaking their heads and saying they'd lost the trail. Sure enough there were so many tracks around the waterhole no one could make sense of them. It looked like every cow, kangaroo and brumby from miles around had come there to drink.

"Right then," said Superintendent Sadleir, looking at his pocket watch. "It must be time for lunch."

Superintendent Nicolson nodded, ordering me to unpack the picnic baskets.

I reckon we got within spitting distance of the Kellys today. Those natives knew they'd be first in line if we walked into an ambush. They led us astray. Sadleir and Nicolson were no better. When it came down to it, they were more interested in saving their skins than catching the Kellys.

Senior Constable Charles Johnson, Violet Town

In Fear

Ned could have chosen to head to New South Wales, even to try to get out of the country, perhaps to make a new life in America, but he didn't. While his mother was in jail, Ned still had a job to do. He wouldn't be going anywhere until she was freed. Most of the time that the gang was on the run, they were no more than 50 kilometres from the Kelly home at Greta.

After the Stringybark Creek killings, Ned and his mates were no doubt expecting to be hounded down by a vengeful police force and outraged public. Yet the police force in Victoria, along with most of the general population, were terrified of the Kelly Gang. Though the number of police in North Eastern Victoria was almost doubled, they showed a definite reluctance to go anywhere near places the gang was suspected of being.

Close Shave

The Kelly Gang was very lucky. In the early hours of the morning, 36 hours after the killings, the gang was seen trying to find a way across the flooded Ovens River by Constable Bracken, who knew the Kellys. News of the killings hadn't yet reached the constable. He waited until the telegraph office opened the next morning before he reported the sighting. By the time troopers arrived, the gang had slipped away.

This wasn't the only close call. Four days later, local police were hot on the outlaws' trail. As torrential rain continued to fall and the floodwaters rose, the gang continually found their way blocked by lagoons. With the police right on their tail, the waters had cut them off and they were trapped on an island surrounded by flooded land. The gang were forced to dismount and let their horses go, while they themselves waded into the water to hide in some reeds. Standing up to their necks in water, with their guns wet and useless, they held their breath as the unsuspecting group of policemen rode by. The gang then rounded up their horses and as darkness fell, they risked lighting a small fire to dry themselves and their guns.

They eventually crossed the flooded Ovens River, but this involved a daring dash through the town of Wangaratta in the dead of night. Little did they know that 22 troopers, brought in for the search and due to start searching the following day, were sleeping in a local hotel. Once again, the gang were seen, this time by local farmers. From the direction they were heading in, it looked like they were planning to take cover in the Warby Ranges.

Top Brass

So far Ned and his friends had had luck on their side. But as police officers moved in from around Victoria, they also had something else on their side – the unintentional help of incompetent and cowardly senior police officers.

Top-ranking policemen were sent to head the hunt for the Kelly Gang. Superintendent Nicolson had been put in charge of the search. Superintendent Sadleir, head of the North Eastern Victoria police district, joined him. The Chief Commissioner of Police, Captain Standish, came up from Melbourne to take part in the search. Inspector Brooke Smith from Beechworth was also called in.

> **"... a parcel of big ugly fat-necked wombat headed big bellied magpie legged narrow hipped splaw-footed sons of Irish Bailiffs or English landlords which is better known as Officers of Justice or Victorian Police..."**
> Ned's opinion of the police, Jerilderie Letter

Brooke Smith was one of the policemen who had been sleeping in the hotel when the gang crept through Wangaratta. The next morning, when an excited constable told him the news of a Kelly Gang sighting right in Wangaratta, Inspector Brooke Smith didn't see any need to rush off immediately. In fact it was two days before the inspector and his party were ready to set out after the gang. Even then they didn't head for the Warby Ranges, but further north.

Inspector Brooke Smith was never in a hurry to get after the Kelly Gang. He didn't like getting up early in the morning. It sometimes took his men more than four hours to get him out of bed. At other times they'd leave without him and he'd catch up with them after lunch. He didn't like camping out in the bush either. Even when, by pure luck, they came across fresh tracks, he insisted on going back to his comfortable hotel in Wangaratta for the night. By the time they rode back to the tracks the following morning, the Kellys were long gone.

"...that article that reminds me of a poodle dog half clipped in the lion fashion, called Brooke E. Smith Superintendent of Police he knows as much about commanding Police as Captain Standish does about mustering mosquitoes and boiling them down for their fat..."
Ned's opinion of Brooke Smith, Jerilderie Letter

Rats' Castle Fiasco

Superintendents Sadleir and Nicolson didn't do much better. Information had been received from a man who was "not quite sober" that the Kellys were hiding in hills near Beechworth. Even though this information was unreliable and five days old, a search of the rocky area, known locally as Rats' Castle, was planned.

Neither Sadleir nor Nicolson wanted to take charge of the raid and each led separate groups of men. They had no firm plan, but thought that the Kellys might be sleeping in a hut in the area and if they struck before dawn they could capture them.

The police assembled in the dark. The Chief Commissioner, Captain Standish, joined the company as did enthusiastic local men, all keen to go down in history as the men who caught the Kellys. Some newspaper reporters from Melbourne also joined the search party which by now was nearly 50 strong.

Under cover of darkness, they raided three huts, but the noise of so many horses could be heard for miles around. Even if the gang had been there, the thunder of approaching horses' hooves would have given them plenty of warning.

Captain Standish, the Chief Commissioner of Police, emigrated to Australia using a false name to escape gambling debts in England. He continued to be addicted to gambling in the colonies. He once lost six months salary in one night.

The officers questioned the people who lived in the huts. A crowd of spectators grew, as neighbours and men mining in the area came to see what all the fuss was about. By this time it was morning and everyone was hungry. Refreshments were sent for and everyone settled down to a pleasant breakfast in the bush. The police decided that the day's search was over and the searchers went back to Beechworth.

Renewed Confidence

After two months on the run, Ned was confident that the gang could evade the bungling police forever. He didn't like being continually dependent on the charity of poor farmers for food, though. He needed money. The Kelly Gang had already run rings around one symbol of authority – the police. Next they would take on the banks.

In 1878, a policeman's uniform included an "English bobby" style helmet and white gloves. Each policeman was issued with a sword.

A Perfect Plan

What if you were there...

It's in all the papers. I saw it all. I'll remember it as long as I live.

I was out in the back yard hanging out the last of the washing – some of the baby's things and the doilies – when one strong hand grabbed my arm and another one clamped over my mouth.

"Don't be afraid," said a voice behind me. "We're sticking up the bank, but you've nothing to fear if you do as I say."

I couldn't see who it was.

"We're going into the house," he said. "Will you stay quiet?"

I nodded. I couldn't have cried out if I'd have

wanted to, I was that frightened.

He led me to the house. My knees were shaking so much I thought I was going to faint and the robber had to half carry me to the back door.

"Is it the Kelly Gang?" I asked, my voice shaking as much as my knees.

"Yes," he said. "I'm Dan Kelly."

It wasn't until we were inside that I could see my captor. I'd been expecting a rough looking lout, but there was a neat, clean-shaven young man standing in front of me.

"Are you all right?" he asked.

I nodded.

"My brother is up the front relieving your master of the bank's money," he said with a smile. "We'll just wait here until he gives the word."

I thought that bushrangers would wear horrible dirty clothes that smelt of horse sweat, but Dan Kelly was wearing a beautiful suit of clothing: grey tweed trousers and vest, a crisp, clean shirt and a black jacket with a white kerchief in the breast pocket. He wore a white hat, which he took off as soon as he was inside the house. His hair was black and quite long, but neatly combed. He smelt nice too. He could see I was frightened, so he fetched me a glass of water and asked me about my family.

After a while, two other robbers came in from the bank chamber with Mr Scott. One of the robbers was Ned Kelly himself. The other I recognised as Stephen Hart, who used to be at the same school as me. Mr Scott was trying to be brave and forbade them from going into the family's rooms. Ned Kelly pushed him aside and went in anyway. Mrs Scott was very calm. You'd think she got held up by bushrangers every day.

They'd collected all the money from the bank. I thought that was the end of it, but the Kellys had other plans. Next thing they took us to carts and wagons in the yard and drove us off. There was quite a crowd, what with the whole Scott family, the bank clerks, the nanny and me.

I was in a cart sitting between Mr Scott and Ned Kelly. The other carts were following. Stephen Hart rode behind. I turned and Dan, who was driving the hawker's wagon, winked to reassure me. I had no clue where we were going, but I'd lost my fear – this was a better way to spend an afternoon than doing the ironing.

We arrived at Faithfull's Creek homestead, which was where the gang was hiding out. The housekeeper cooked a meal and we were invited to eat in the kitchen with the bushrangers. While Ned Kelly was impressing Mrs Scott and the other ladies with his stories, I talked to Dan. He told me about the hard times they'd had since they'd been on the run and how his poor mother was in jail.

Then at about half past nine, Ned suddenly said, "It's time to go, lads." I asked Dan if I could have a souvenir to remember him by. He gave me a brand new sixpence from the money they stole from the bank and a bullet which he carved with his initials. Then they rode off in a cloud of dust and that was the last I ever saw of Dan Kelly.

Fanny Shaw, maid

Thoughtful Thieves

Ned knew that he would need the support of friends and relatives in the district if the gang were going to remain free. He also knew that he was asking a lot of these people. Another section of the Felons Apprehension Act stated that there would be very harsh penalties for anyone who helped the Kellys. Prison sentences of up to 15 years hard labour were promised.

The gang had a reputation as callous murderers because of the events at Stringybark Creek. Ned wanted to change the public's opinion of them. They had already tried to show that although they were outlaws they were no threat to ordinary people. They had paid for food they demanded from stores and hotels. In one case, when they didn't have money, they went back weeks later to pay for it. They needed money badly, but Ned was determined they wouldn't be like other bushrangers, bailing up people on the road and demanding their money. They would only steal from the banks. And the Kelly Gang bank robberies would be like no others.

The area where the Kellys operated is known today, as it was at the time of the outbreak, as Kelly Country. Kelly Country is the area of North Eastern Victoria from Euroa in the west to Beechworth in the east, from Mansfield in the south to the Murray River in the north.

A Cunning Plan

Ned decided to "stick up" the National Bank of Australia in the town of Euroa. He'd given the matter a lot of thought. The bank was on the edge of the town, away from the main street. And a few kilometres away there was a property called Faithfull's Creek, which he could use as headquarters. Rich squatters who lived in the city owned it. This suited his needs perfectly.

People in small towns were in a state of panic about further Kelly Gang attacks. One man, on hearing a sudden bang during the night, rushed outside and hid up a tree. He stayed there until morning, when he discovered it had just been his cook dropping a saucepan.

Ned and Joe Byrne tried to think of everything they would need and everything that could go wrong. They worked on their plan until they thought it was flawless. On Tuesday, 10 December 1878, a funeral was taking place in Euroa as well as a hotel-licensing meeting. Many of the townsfolk would be taking part in either one of these events. That was the day the Kelly Gang would rob the bank.

Best-dressed Bushrangers

The robbery was to be no hit-and-run affair. The gang didn't want to ride into town, guns blazing, steal the money and gallop off again. This would result in an immediate response to track them down. They wanted it to be a quiet business, unnoticed by the townspeople, so that they would have plenty of time to get away before the alarm was raised.

The first thing they did was hold up the homestead at Faithfull's Creek the day before they intended to rob the bank. They rounded up the farm workers and locked them in a storehouse. The people working on the farm assumed the Kelly Gang had come to rob them, but they hadn't. They planned to launch the robbery from there.

James Gloster, a travelling salesman, arrived soon after the gang. He was a regular visitor to the area selling clothing and household goods from the back of his wagon. The gang locked him in the storeroom with the other men while they sorted through his wares looking for new clothing. It seemed as if Gloster had unwittingly stumbled into the middle of a bank robbery. But it was no accident. It was prearranged. Gloster was a friend of the Kellys. Each gang member selected an outfit from among the hawker's stock – everything fitted perfectly. Ned didn't want his gang looking like a bunch of ruffians. Ned selected brown tweed trousers and vest, a blue coat and a felt hat. He completed his outfit with a pink tie. Dan chose an outfit similar to his brother's. The other two preferred suits – Joe's light grey, Steve's dark grey. They all put white handkerchiefs in their jacket pockets and splashed on some cologne. Then they were ready – the best- dressed bushrangers ever seen.

They spent the night at the homestead and the following day they cut the telegraph wires leading to Euroa. A party of passing kangaroo hunters and a man who came to fix the telegraph wires joined the prisoners in the storehouse. The gang borrowed Gloster's wagon and the hunters' cart and rode into town, leaving Joe to watch the prisoners.

A Stick-up

It was some time after 4 p.m. when the gang rode sedately into the deserted town. The bank was closed. Ned knocked on the door asking to see the bank manager. When the bank teller refused to let him enter, Ned pushed his way in. Steve was close behind him. They both drew revolvers and Ned asked the manager to hand over the money. Meanwhile Dan had gone round the back in case anyone tried to get away. They collected over £2000 worth of coins, banknotes and gold. They were disappointed. They had hoped there would be much more than that.

Ned didn't want news of the robbery to spread too

soon, so he took the bank manager and his employees as prisoners. As the bank manager lived behind the bank, Ned also had to round up his wife, seven children, mother-in-law and two servants. Borrowing another cart to carry this crowd, the gang made their way back to the homestead at Faithfull's Creek. They had something to eat, let their prisoners out for some exercise and entertained them with a show of their trick riding skills. When it grew dark, they told their captives to give them three hours start before they let anyone know what had happened, then they disappeared into the night.

"No doubt I am now placed in very peculiar circumstances and you might blame me for it but if you knew how I have been wronged and persecuted you would say I cannot be blamed."

Ned thinks he has been wronged, Cameron Letter

A Red Letter

During the day-and-a-half spent at the homestead, as well as guarding the prisoners, Joe Byrne had been busy with another task. Ned believed that if only people knew the truth about his lifehow the police had hounded his family, the innocence of his mother–then they would understand why he'd been driven to bushranging. Ned had previously dictated a long and rambling letter to Joe who, being the one with the best handwriting, wrote it down. In Joe's spare time at the homestead, he made two neat copies of the letter in red ink. Ned posted one to a politician in Melbourne by the name of Donald Cameron and the other to Superintendent Sadleir. The first letter has survived and is now known as the Cameron Letter.

Public Relations

In the following days, newspapers all over the country were full of details of the bank robbery. The mood of the reporters had changed. They were impressed by the skill and care that had gone into the planning of the robbery. They called it "audacious" and "daring" and said it was more like something that had happened in a novel than a real event. The released prisoners told how they had been treated well. The women reported how polite the young men had been, and how well dressed. The police, who were still busy searching in other parts of the colony, were spoken of less kindly.

> **"It seems impossible for me to get any justice without I make a statement to someone that will take notice of it, as it is no use in me complaining about anything that the Police may choose to say or swear against me and the public in their ignorance and blindness will undoubtedly back them up to their utmost."**
> Ned's lack of faith in police justice, Cameron Letter

There was one disappointment for Ned. The

police had forbidden newspapers to publish his letter. Reporters had quoted bits from the letter though. It was better than nothing.

Ned's plan had worked perfectly. Not only had they robbed the bank and got clean away, they had also started to change people's opinions of the Kelly Gang. In what we would today call a "public relations exercise", Ned had made a conscious effort to get people to like him. The public no longer thought of him as a rough, uncouth bushranger, but a clever, smartly dressed man. His PR exercise had been a complete success.

Puzzling Pursuit

A magistrate had noticed the broken telegraph wires as he'd passed Faithfull's Creek on the train earlier that day. He got off the train at Benalla to alert the police. Superintendents Nicolson and Sadleir immediately swung into action. But instead of heading straight for Faithfull's Creek, they jumped on the train and set out in the opposite direction! An informant had told them that the Kellys were on their way to New South Wales. They decided to act on this information. At the time, the gang were still at the Faithfull's Creek homestead, just 45 kilometres away, and would have been an easy target. Once again, luck and police bungling were on Ned's side.

The Kelly Gang did cross the Murray River into New South Wales, but not for another two months. They weren't escaping from the Victorian police or looking for a place to hide. They were on their way to hold up another bank.

Two policemen who took part in the hunt for the Kellys. They wore ordinary clothes so that people didn't know they were police.

The Kelly Gang Strikes Again

What if you were there...

Some foolish people are saying it was the most exciting thing to ever happen in this town. Other misguided fools are declaring it will put Jerilderie on the map and make it famous forever. Some think it is amusing. I am not amused. It is an outrage.

I'd just ridden home from Urana, a gruelling 40-mile ride in fearfully hot weather. It was 22 minutes to five when I arrived home. I dismounted in the paddock behind the parson's house and left my horse to feed and water itself. I trudged wearily to my own home behind the bank and went straight to the bathroom as I was in urgent need of a plunge bath. I had just filled the bath and was about to commence removing my dusty clothing when Mr Living, the bank's accountant, appeared at the door.

"We're held up, sir," he said. "It's the Kellys."

I was not in the mood for humorous nonsense. "What rubbish," I replied, ordering him to get himself back to the bank chamber immediately while I attended to my bath.

"It's not rubbish," said a rough-accented voice. "We want your key to the safe."

I turned and there was a young man with a most insolent expression on his face and a revolver in each hand, both pointed in my direction. Thus I was persuaded that Living was not joking.

The safe in my bank is opened using two keys – one of which is in my possession, the other in the possession of Mr Living. The long, hot ride had not left me in a good humour. I knew there was no possibility that I could foil the robbers' evil intentions, but I could at least delay them.

"I will finish my bath first, if it's all the same to you," I said and shut the door in the bushranger's face.

I completed my toilet, put on some trousers, a silk bathrobe and my smoking cap. Feeling refreshed, I was escorted to the Royal Mail Hotel next door to the bank. There I made the acquaintance of Ned Kelly, who immediately demanded that I open the safe. Though it vexed me sorely, I had no choice but to do as he asked. The outlaws grasped at the bags of money and also some jewellery, which was being held for safekeeping. Kelly then pulled out a number of documents – deeds, mortgages and the like – which were also in the safe. He set light to them while he ranted about banks being the enemy of the poor.

The outlaws seemed disappointed by the amount of money kept in the bank and searched for more. Once they were persuaded that they had it all, they escorted Living and myself back to the Royal Mail and bought us all a drink. I at first declined, but then thought a drop of spirits might steel my nerves should an opportunity to overpower the outlaws arise.

Their vile deed was done, but they seemed in no hurry to leave our town. Kelly saw fit to make a speech to his prisoners, now some 30-odd people, and lectured us about how the police had mistreated him and left him no choice but to murder three of their number. Then he announced we could all leave if we liked.

Still the outlaws seemed in no rush to depart. I caught the eye of the junior clerk and told him to fetch my horse. By this time the crowd was dispersing and Kelly was out in the street talking to Reverend Gribble. Ensuring that no one was watching, I went round the back of the hotel where the clerk was holding my horse.

"I shall ride like the wind," I told him. "They'll never catch me."

Mr John Tarleton, Bank Manager, Jerilderie

Another Robbery

The already saddle-sore bank manager rode another 92 kilometres to Deniliquin to raise the alarm. He didn't get there until 6 a.m. the following day. Once again the slow communications of the time meant that the Kelly Gang had plenty of time to make their leisurely escape.

"If I had robbed and plundered ravished and murdered everything I met young and old rich and poor, the public could not do any more than take firearms and Assisting the police as they have done."

Ned feels the public is against him, Jerilderie Letter

The £2000 that they had stolen from the Euroa bank didn't last long. It was a small fortune in 1878, but Ned had generously shared the money with his family and friends and by February the gang needed more funds.

Confident after the success of the last bank hold-up and the grudging praise it had brought from the press, Ned had a plan for another bank robbery. This one was even more daring than the last.

Counterfeit Troopers

He chose the Bank of New South Wales in the town of Jerilderie. The bank was in the heart of the main street. The gang planned to size up the town on Sunday and rob the bank on Monday. For their headquarters, instead of a remote homestead, Ned chose the police station.

The gang held up the Jerilderie police station in the early hours of Sunday, 9 February 1879. They soon had the town's two policemen safely locked in their own jail and had made themselves comfortable in Constable Devine's family quarters.

The gang was so confident of their success that they didn't even feel they had to hide. Joe and Steve dressed up in spare police uniforms and rode around the town with the other policeman, Constable Richards. Townspeople thought they were new policemen being shown around the town. They didn't realise that they were members of the feared Kelly Gang who were familiarising themselves with the town so that they could work out the best way to rob the bank.

"The Queen must surely be proud of such heroic men as the Police and Irish soldiers as It takes eight or eleven of the biggest mud crushers in Melbourne to take one poor little half starved larrikin to a watch house."
Ned's view of police as cowardly, Jerilderie Letter

The following morning Joe and Dan, dressed in police uniform, had time to buy some meat at the butcher's and have their horses reshod. Then Ned put on police uniform. He held up the publican in the hotel next door to the bank, telling him he wanted the use of his bar parlour for a few hours. He would hold the prisoners there.

Easy Money

Joe and Ned then held up the bank. The bank manager wasn't present, but they took the bank clerks to the "prison" in the bar next door. Dan kept guard over them and anyone else who happened to come into the hotel.

When the bank manager returned, he was filling his bath when he found Steve Hart pointing a gun at him and demanding his key to the safe. Ned was again disappointed by the amount of money at the bank – just over £2000.

"I give fair warning to all those who has reason to fear me to sell out and give £10 out of every hundred towards the widow and orphan fund and do not attempt to reside in Victoria... I am a widow's son outlawed and my orders must be obeyed."
Closing words of the Jerilderie Letter

As an afterthought, Ned sent some of the townspeople to chop down the telegraph poles.

Publicity Campaign

Ned had a new, longer letter which he and Joe had written. Since he had had no luck writing to a politician, and the police had forbidden the press to print his letter, Ned needed a new way of getting his case heard. He wanted his new letter to be printed on handbills which would be circulated by the people themselves. This way, he thought, he could reach as many people as possible.

Like someone today who wants their grievances aired on a TV current affairs show, Ned believed that if the facts were known, people would understand that he had been forced to break the law.

Ned had hoped that the town's newspaper editor would print his 56-page letter. He was annoyed when he discovered that the editor had found out that they were in town and had escaped. Instead Ned gave the letter to Mr Living, the bank's accountant, who promised to give it to the editor. But Living didn't keep his promise. Instead, he handed it over to the police. This second letter is known as the Jerilderie Letter.

The authorities made a copy of Ned's Jerilderie Letter, but the original disappeared sometime after 1913. It resurfaced again in 2000 and is now held at the State Library of Victoria.

Unhurried Getaway

Even though they knew at least two people had ridden out of town to raise the alarm, the gang still didn't seem to be in a hurry to leave. They collected the money and went back to the hotel, where they bought drinks for their prisoners. Leaving the two policemen locked in their cell, Ned let the other prisoners leave. He stole a horse and a saddle, while Steve took the parson's watch. When the owners complained about these thefts, Ned promptly gave them back again. Then they finally left town.

Reign of Terror

The bank robberies at Euroa and Jerilderie make interesting and, at times, amusing tales. But for people at the time, living in small remote towns with only one or two policemen to protect them, it wasn't so amusing. They were afraid of the Kellys.

The police seemed powerless to capture them. The gang had killed three men. Though they had never killed any civilians, Ned had made a number of dire threats to do so. People thought that they would be safe as long as they surrendered quickly and willingly. They practised putting up their hands until they could do it as quickly as possible. Travellers along country roads made sure that they had their hands ready to raise if they were held up.

Ned's wish to have his letter printed and distributed for everyone to read eventually came true—but not until 50 years after his death. It is now posted on the Internet and has been read by millions of people, not only in Australia, but around the world.

If newspaper readers around the country were eagerly waiting for the next daring and entertaining Kelly Gang exploit, they were disappointed. After Ned and his boys disappeared into the bush after the Jerilderie hold-up, it was almost a year-and-a-half before they were seen again.

Disappearing Outlaws

What if you were there...

We've been camped in these freezing hills for nearly two weeks. I'm sick of it. Two weeks of sleeping during the day and then creeping out like thieves in the night to watch over the homes of the Kellys' sympathisers. The Superintendent seems to think that sooner or later the Kellys won't be able to resist the lure of home and we'll be able to nab them. The trouble is the Kellys are cleverer than the senior police.

We are watching Maggie Skilling's house. That's Ned's eldest sister. She's just about the head of the family now, what with her brothers on the run and her husband and mother in jail for the Fitzpatrick business. She looks after her land, her children and her younger brothers and sisters. We're pretty sure she feeds her outlaw brothers and their mates as well.

I don't sleep well in the daylight. Yesterday was as bad as ever. Every time I woke with a rock in my side or the sun on my head, I'd smell bread baking. She's got a lot of mouths to feed, has Maggie, but by the smell of it, this batch of loaves was for an even bigger crowd.

Last night, I was wet through from sitting out in a fine drizzle. The light had gone out in the house at about 10 o'clock, so I'd spent the hours of the night staring at darkness. Then at about four in the morning I noticed some movement – a single figure creeping out of the door and going over to the horses. I nudged Constable Mills next to me who, though he swears he wasn't, was asleep. There was no moon, so it was hard to make out, but I could see that the figure was carrying heavy bags and heading to the horse paddock.

Whoever it was saddled one of the horses and mounted. We crept over to our horses and followed at a safe distance.

"This is it," I whispered to Mills. "They're taking food to the Kellys."

It was hard tailing the horse what with there being no moon. After an hour I thought I'd lost them. Then suddenly we came out of the trees. The horse and rider were on the other side of a clearing. I held my horse still, hoping we hadn't been seen, but it was too late. The rider spurred the horse which galloped off.

The chase was on then. We were gaining a little. The rider's hat blew back and I could see long black hair stream out. She was wearing trousers and riding astride like a man, but I knew for sure it was Maggie Skilling and her saddle bags were stuffed full of food for her brothers.

Just as we thought we were going to catch her, she disappeared. Mills and I split up. I went up a ravine, while Mills followed another track. The ravine was steep and narrow, but there was no sign of her. The first light of the morning was just starting to smear the horizon. A terrible thought came to me. What exactly was I going to do if I suddenly came across the Kellys' camp? If they were waiting at the end of this ravine, I'd be a sitting duck. I couldn't possibly manage four men by myself. Just then a rider came up behind me. I turned, pulling my gun. Lucky I didn't fire. It was Mills. The track he had followed had petered out. With guns drawn, we rode on without a word. All I could hear was the pounding of my heart. We rode up that narrow gap for an hour, always feeling that every moment could be our last. Then the track skirted around a large fallen rock and there in front of us was Maggie Skilling. She was sitting on a log with her thumbs pressed into her cheeks, her fingers waggling and her tongue stuck out.

"G'day, boys," she said. "Out for some early morning air?"

I quickly glanced around. She seemed to be on her own. I dismounted and went to inspect her bulging saddlebags. If we couldn't have the Kellys, we'd have Maggie on suspicion of aiding and abetting outlaws. I undid the buckles and pulled out the contents. The bags, both of them, were stuffed with tablecloths. When she saw my face, Maggie laughed till tears ran down her face.

Jim Dixon, volunteer Kelly hunter

The Legend Grows

Soon after the Jerilderie hold-up, the reward for capture of the gang increased in both Victoria and New South Wales. There was now an unbelievable total of £8000 reward. This amount is the equivalent today of around $2 million. The fact that no one was ever tempted to give the Kellys away is an indication of the support they had. The gang's exploits were already starting to move into the realm of legend. Songs were written about them and sung to the tunes of traditional Irish songs by their sympathisers and admirers. Joe Byrne, a man who was "for a bushman clever with his pen" is said to have written at least one of the ballads himself.

V. R.

£8000 REWARD

ROBBERY and MURDER.

WHEREAS EDWARD KELLY, DANIEL KELLY, STEPHEN HART and JOSEPH BYRNE have been declared OUTLAWS in the Colony of Victoria, and whereas warrants have been issued charging the aforesaid men with the WILFUL MURDER of MICHAEL SCANLON, Police Constable of the Colony of VICTORIA, and whereas the above-named offenders are STILL at LARGE, and have recently committed divers felonies in the Colony of NEW SOUTH WALES; Now, therefore, I, SIR HERCULES GEORGE ROBERT ROBINSON, the GOVERNOR, do, by this, my proclamation issued with the advice of the Executive Council, hereby notify that a REWARD of £4,000 will be paid, three-fourths by the Government of NEW SOUTH WALES, and one fourth by certain Banks trading in the Colony, for the apprehension of the above-named Four Offenders, or a reward of £1000 for the apprehension of any one of them; and that, in ADDITION to the above reward, a similar REWARD of £4000 has been offered by the Government of VICTORIA, and I further notify that the said REWARD will be equitably apportioned between any persons giving information which shall lead to the apprehension of the offenders and any members of the police force or other persons who may actually effect such apprehension or assist thereat.

(Signed) HENRY PARKES,
Colonial Secretary, New South Wales.

(Signed) BRYAN O'LOGHLEN,
Attorney General, Victoria.

Dated 15th February, 1879.

A reward poster offering £8000 for the capture of the Kelly Gang.

On the Run

Life on the run must have been a strange ghost-like experience for the gang. They still never strayed far from home, but they were constantly on the move. They travelled up to 100 kilometres in a day – or rather in a night, for the gang always travelled at night. During the day they played cards and tried to get some sleep.

Their friends and families saw to it that they were well fed. Ned's sister, Maggie Skilling, was their biggest supporter. A cooking fire could have easily given the gang's hiding place away. So that they didn't have to make a fire, Maggie baked bread, cooked meals and rode through the night to take the food to her brothers.

It wasn't a comfortable life. The gang may not have gone hungry, but they suffered from lack of sleep and from boredom.

Counter Attack

The police were having no luck at all finding the outlaws. They decided that this was because their friends and relatives were too ready to help them. Even though they closely watched the Kelly house, Ned's sisters still managed to outfox them. The police were getting more and more criticism from the press. Chief Commissioner Standish decided that he would attack the Kelly sympathisers.

Twenty-one friends and relatives of the gang were arrested and kept imprisoned without trial for months. But this didn't have the effect that Captain Standish wanted. Not all of the men arrested were really Kelly sympathisers. The families of the arrested men were left short-handed on their farms. Instead of discouraging people from supporting the Kelly Gang, this ill-treatment only made people more sympathetic to their cause.

"They used to rush into the house upset all the milk dishes break tins of eggs empty the flour out of the bags onto the ground...and shove the girls in front of them into the rooms like dogs so as if anyone was there they would shoot the girls first..."
Police ill-treatment of Ned's sisters, Jerilderie Letter

Captain Standish's next step caused even more discomfort to poor people. Anyone suspected of helping the Kellys was banned from taking up new land selections. This was perhaps the worse thing he could have done. Right from the beginning Ned had been complaining that greedy, rich people prevented poor people from taking up land. The police commissioner was only proving Ned right. The troopers did pick on innocent poor people. The Kelly Gang's support continued to grow.

Double Agent

While friends and relatives spied on the police and let the gang know what they were up to, the police were trying to find people to spy for them. One man they approached seemed willing to do the job. His name was Aaron Sherritt. He had been Joe Byrne's good friend for many years and he had been with the gang in their stock-stealing days. Some policemen didn't believe that he would really betray his friends.

> **"I dont think there is a man born could have the patience to suffer it as long as I did or ever allow his blood to get cold while such insults as these were unavenged and yet in every paper that is printed I am called the blackest and coldest blooded murderer ever on record. But if I hear any more of it I will not exactly show them what cold blooded murder is but wholesale and retail slaughter."**
> Ned threatens the police,
> Jerilderie Letter

At the same time Aaron was one of the gang's most trusted friends. He gave them information about the police and their movements. Ned had faith in Aaron's loyalty to the gang.

Though Joe and Ned trusted him completely, other friends of the gang were starting to get suspicious. They had heard that Aaron was being paid well by the police for information. With the money from the Jerilderie bank robbery all used up, there was no money coming from the Kelly Gang. Whose side was Aaron really on?

Rumours were spreading that Aaron was threatening to kill Joe. The police fed the rumours and started a dispute between the Sherritt and Byrne families. Eventually Joe was convinced that his friend couldn't be trusted. If he was a traitor, Aaron would have to die. Joe went to Aaron's house and shot his friend dead. There were four policemen hiding in the house at the time, waiting for just such a visit. When they heard the shots fired, they stayed where they were, hiding in the bedroom. Joe rode away and no one followed him.

"This sort of cruelty and disgraceful conduct to my brothers and sisters who had no protection coupled with the conviction of my Mother and those innocent men certainly made my blood boil..."
Ned explains his growing anger with the police, Cameron Letter

Pity the Police

Much has been said about the cowardliness of the police during the Kelly hunt. The senior officers of the police force were unpopular with poor selectors. The officers were wealthy and privileged and on the side of the squatters. Ordinary police were simple men, often Irish like the Kellys, who had been ordered to look after the interests of the squatters before the selectors. They were not well equipped. Their guns were not the best available. After three years training in the artillery corps in Melbourne, recruits were sent to postings all over the colony, so they were not familiar with the area they were working in. They didn't have knowledge of the local geography, unlike the Kellys who knew the bush like the backs of their hands. Many police were from the city, unfamiliar with, even afraid of, the bush.

The policemen cowering in Aaron Sherritt's bedroom had heard the Kelly Gang stories. They knew the Kellys had gunned down their fellow officers when the officers had fought back. They had just witnessed Joe Byrne executing his one-time friend. They knew that if they burst out and attacked the bushrangers standing at the door, there would be bloodshed – more than likely their own.

Circumstances have forced us to become what we are — outcasts and outlaws, and, bad as we are, we are not so bad as we are supposed to be.

Ned thinks the gang doesn't deserve its bad reputation, Letter to Chief Secretary

Literary Inspiration

While the gang was on the run the hours must often have seemed very long. But it seems that one of the things that Ned did to pass the time was to read. Joe was undoubtedly the most well read of the gang, but there is evidence that Ned read as well. Historians claim that one of Ned's favourite books was *Lorna Doone*. This book is about a family of outlaws who terrorised an area in England called Exmoor. They rode around the countryside with their horses laden with plunder and wearing iron plates on their breasts and heads to protect themselves from their enemies. It is believed that Ned got the inspiration for his strangest idea from the pages of books like this and Sir Walter Scott's *Ivanhoe*, a story about a 12th century knight. He decided that for their next exploit, the gang would all wear armour.

My name it is Ned Kelly,
I'm known adversely well.
My ranks are free,
my name is law,
Wherever I do dwell.
My friends are all united,
my mates are lying near.
We sleep beneath these
shady trees,
No danger do we fear.

A verse from the ballad said to be composed by Joe Byrne.

Taken Alive

What if you were there...

The train rattled northwards at a tremendous speed, steaming blindly into the darkness. It was going so fast it seemed it might jump off the rails. I shivered, whether with cold or fear I don't care to say. I was beginning the biggest adventure of my life.

I work at the Argus. *Most of the time I'm running to get sandwiches or grog for the reporters. Sometimes I might get to carry some equipment for the photographer. I'd like to be a pressman myself one day – a crime reporter, at the scene of the crime, interviewing policemen and tearful lady witnesses. One day.*

I was in the copy room last night, just about to go home, when I heard the buzz. A telegram had just arrived from Beechworth. The Kellys were holding up an inn at Glenrowan. A special police train was leaving Melbourne in half an hour. I didn't go home. Instead I ran to the railway station. The engine was just building up steam. When no one was looking, I jumped on the train and hid in the baggage compartment.

We stopped twice along the way to pick up policemen, the last time at Benalla. The train had just picked up speed again, when it suddenly slowed. My legs were cramped, so I got up to walk around and peered out of the window. I could see a strange red light ahead waving back and forth. The engine driver was calling out. I could tell from his voice that he was afraid. I thought, "It's the Kellys. They're holding up the train." The train stopped. A young man with blond hair lowered the candle he had been holding behind a red lady's scarf to get the driver's attention. He was very agitated, shouting something about the Kellys and the line being torn up.

The train started off again, slowly this time.

We didn't go far. In a short time we pulled into Glenrowan station. There was a tremendous noise and clatter as the policemen got their nervous horses out of the horse van. There was so much noise and confusion on the platform that no one noticed when I crept off the train. I thought we'd be in for a long wait, but I had hardly got off the train when I heard the crack of gunfire. I ran in the direction of the sound and soon came across two policemen supporting a tall man who was bleeding from the wrist.

"I've been hit," he was saying. "The very first shot."

The police were taking up positions outside the inn. A voice was shouting from the building. "Fire away, you miserable dogs. You can't hurt us." It was a strange hollow voice. I moved to the side of the inn, where I could see everything but stay well out of the line of fire. The gunfire continued until the night air was thick with smoke. Then a figure emerged from the darkness of the inn's verandah out into the smoky moonlight. I had never seen anything like it before. It was a huge figure. It walked towards the police with an unnatural stiffness. It had a massive head growing from its shoulders. The monster was carrying a gun in each hand and as it advanced, it fired at the police. It banged one revolver on its chest and then on its infernal head. The sound rang out as if some demon were beating an enormous cracked kettle with an iron spoon.

The police shot at the monster, but the bullets just bounced off it. It staggered a little when bullets bounced off its head, only to recover and keep walking. Drops of thick black liquid left a trail behind it.

I froze in fear as the figure changed direction. It was coming towards me. I had an awful feeling it could smell me in the darkness. I crawled through the undergrowth, but the creature kept following me. Then, when it had the cover of a large tree, it sank to the ground. It was no more than two yards away from me. I watched in horror as the monster reached up and removed its huge head. Then I saw that it wasn't a monster at all. It was a man who'd been wearing an iron helmet shaped like an upturned nail can. Beneath the helmet was a bruised and bloody face. In the moonlight, I saw that the liquid trailing from its arm wasn't black, it was dark red. It was blood. It wasn't a monster, it was a human being. It was Ned Kelly himself.

Billy Walsh, errand boy, the *Argus* newspaper

Bush Knights

The armour that the gang made was constructed from ploughshares – the curved blades on ploughs which push back the earth to make furrows. These were made from iron almost a centimetre thick. With the help of willing blacksmiths, four suits of armour were made. They each consisted of a breastplate, a back plate and shoulder guards. The breastplate had a flap of iron strapped to the bottom like an apron to protect the groin. The head was protected by a large cylindrical helmet that rested on the shoulders, covering the face entirely, except for a slit for the eyes.

Ruthless Plan

Ned's third and final plan was different from his other two. This final campaign started with the cold-blooded murder of a one-time friend. Ned knew that once news of Aaron Sherritt's death spread, police would move in on the area. The murder had taken place on a Saturday night. There would be no more trains running until Monday morning. The only train coming up the line would be a special train full of policemen. This was Ned's target. The gang rode to the small town of Glenrowan and took over one of the town's hotels.

Ned's first job at Glenrowan was to take up some of the railway tracks. To do this he needed the help

Kelly Gang armour. This is the helmet and breastplate worn by Ned.

of railway repairmen who were camped close by. The section of track they chose was at the top of a steep gully. It seemed that the gang was planning to derail the train and send it, and the police inside, crashing to the bottom.

Ned was expecting that the police hiding in Aaron's hut would raise the alarm immediately. They didn't. They stayed hidden in the hut until daylight. Even then, well-meaning supporters of the Kelly Gang stopped messengers riding with the news to Beechworth. In the past, the slow response of the police had helped the gang. This time it was to lead to their undoing.

Fun and Games

The gang made themselves comfortable at the Glenrowan Inn and waited for the train. Meanwhile they were collecting up a crowd of prisoners. As well as the railway repairmen, there was the stationmaster and his family, the schoolteacher and his family and the town's one policeman, Constable Bracken. Throughout the following day, the number of prisoners swelled to over 60. Ned looked after his "guests" in his usual way. To stop them getting bored he organised dancing and sports competitions. All of the Kelly Gang joined in these activities.

One of the prisoners taught Ned the steps to a dance called the quadrille. As they were in a hotel, there was also a great deal of drinking. The prisoners enjoyed the outlaws' hospitality late into the night.

The train was overdue. Ned let some of his prisoners go home, including the schoolteacher, Thomas Curnow, who Ned had grown to trust during the course of the night. It was after 2 a.m. – now more than 24 hours since Aaron's death. The gang hadn't had any sleep for two nights. Ned was beginning to think that the police train was never coming. He had just told the remaining 40-odd prisoners they could go home, when he heard a train whistle. The prisoners were ushered back into the hotel and locked in. The gang then got into their armour.

> **If my life teaches the public that men are made mad by bad treatment, and if the police are taught that they may not exasperate to madness men they persecute and ill treat, my life will not be entirely thrown away.**
> **Interview while in** Beechworth Prison, the Age, 9 August 1880

Trust Betrayed

Instead of steaming through the town to its destruction, the train had stopped at Glenrowan station. The schoolteacher, Thomas Curnow, had not gone home, but had gone instead to warn the train. Constable Bracken escaped from the hotel and ran to tell the police of the Kelly Gang's murderous plans. On the train was a troop of 24 police and trackers led by Superintendent Hare, the policeman now in charge of the Kelly Hunt. The police quickly got off the train and surrounded the hotel. The gang were on the verandah shrouded in darkness.

I do not pretend that I have led a blameless life, or that one fault justifies another, but the public in judging a case like mine should remember that the darkest life may have a bright side, and that after the worst has been said against a man, he may, if he is heard, tell a story in his own rough way that will perhaps lead them to intimate the harshness of their thoughts against him, and find as many excuses for him as he would plead for himself.
Interview while in Beechworth Prison, the Age, 9 August 1880

Ned fired the first shot. It hit Superintendent Hare in the wrist. The commander of the assault fainted and was taken away to Benalla for treatment. From the first moments, the police were without a leader.

Ned moved out from the verandah into the moonlight. Sleep deprived, possibly having drunk too much whisky, he walked out in front of the police, believing that his armour would protect him. This was the first the police had seen of Ned in his armour. It was a frightening sight. They couldn't work out what it was that was prowling around in the moonlight with a gun in each hand. Ned wore a long oilskin coat over the top of his armour adding to his unearthly appearance. Some police thought it was a ghost, others a madman. Whatever it was, they fired at it. Their shots seemed to bounce off the weird creature. Perhaps it was the devil himself.

The armour made Ned feel invincible, but it only protected him where it covered his body. His legs and arms were unprotected.

Bloodshed

Ned was soon hit in his left arm and in his right foot. Just as the police leader had been, the Kelly Gang's leader was seriously wounded in the first minutes of the gunfight.

The police were firing furiously at the inn without a thought for the unfortunate prisoners inside. Women and children were screaming. There were not only screams of fear, but terrible screams of pain. Four civilians were shot in the volley of police fire, including two children. Three of these victims died from their wounds. Joe was also hit in the leg. After Joe was shot, he retreated with Dan and Steve into the inn for cover. Ned,

When Ned's pockets were searched, they were found to contain a lady's watch, two gold chains, some ammunition and a threepence.The doctor tending to Ned's wounds took off his armour and discovered that around his waist he was wearing a green silk sash with a gold fringe. It was the sash he had been awarded for rescuing Dick Shelton from drowning when he was only 11 years old.

bleeding badly and in a state of shock, continued to wander around outside.

In a lull in the firing, the terrified women and children tried to escape. They called to police not to fire, but their pleas were ignored and a hail of bullets drove them back. A bullet grazed a baby's head.

Towards dawn, Sergeant Steele arrived from Wangaratta with more police. He leapt off his horse, eager to get into the fight. As the hostages tried again to make their escape, the overzealous Steele fired wildly at them, even though other police tried to stop him. Another civilian, a young man of 18, was wounded.

Ned was losing an enormous amount of blood. He limped back to the hotel and arrived to see his best friend Joe shot dead. Believing that Dan and Steve had escaped, Ned found a horse to make his own escape. Weak from loss of blood and weighed down by his armour, he couldn't mount the horse.

Death in the Morning

Ned called out to Dan and heard a faint reply from the inn. He realised his mistake. His brother and Steve Hart were still in the hotel. The police continued to shoot at Ned, wounding him again and again as he tried to make his way back to the inn to rescue Dan and Steve. As he staggered to the cover of a fallen tree, the police called out for him to surrender, but he refused.

Finally a shot in the leg brought Ned crashing to the ground. The police rushed to overcome him, grabbing his revolver. With 28 wounds in his body and after bleeding for more than four hours, Ned was unable to fight back. The police took off the helmet and only then realised they had captured Ned Kelly himself. Sergeant Steele moved in to finish him off, but Constable Bracken stopped him. Ned was carried away and into custody.

By this time, Superintendent Sadleir had arrived from Benalla. Surely now, with proper leadership, the police would finish the matter swiftly. But that was not the case. The next morning the last of the prisoners finally got away from the inn. There were now 50 policemen against two outlaws. Still the police waited. Sadleir ordered a cannon to be sent up from Melbourne to attack the tiny weatherboard inn. The inn was silent. Neither Dan nor Steve were returning fire. Still Sadleir waited.

When Joe Byrne's body was searched, he was found to be carrying a prayer book in one pocket and a brown paper bag of poison in the other. On his fingers, he wore the rings belonging to Michael Scanlon, one of the policemen killed at Stringybark Creek.

At about three in the afternoon, Constable Johnson ran out of patience with his superior officer. He pointed out that a splash of kerosene and a match would quickly do as much damage as a cannon to the flimsy wooden building. He calmly walked forward and set light to the inn. Timid to the last, the other police still stayed back.

Hundreds of people had gathered to watch the drama unfold. They cheered as a priest strode forward and entered the burning building. He saw Joe dead in the bar. In a back room he found Dan and Steve, also lying dead on the floor. He called out the news to the police who just had time to pull Joe's body from the flames. The inn, with a calico ceiling and paper-lined walls, was a firetrap. It was destroyed in a few minutes.

Newspaper reporters tied Joe's dead body to a door so that photos could be taken. Postcards carrying photos of the dead bushranger were sold as souvenirs.

The bodies of Dan and Steve were burnt beyond recognition. Whether they were shot by police bullets or whether they shot each other to avoid capture, no one knows.

Disaster and Defeat

Ned's first two bold hold-ups had worked like a dream. His third and final plan had turned into a nightmare. Ned was captured. His brother and best friend were killed. Four innocent townspeople also died.

Just what Ned's aim was at Glenrowan is hard to

fathom. The bushrangers had brought a keg of blasting powder and a coil of fuse with them. Witnesses noticed crowds of armed sympathisers gathering during the night. At one stage, Chinese skyrockets were let off as some sort of signal. There was no bank in the small town of Glenrowan. Whatever they were planning, it was more than a simple bank robbery.

After the Glenrowan shoot-out, the suits of Kelly armour became the property of three different organisations and one individual. Historians examined the four suits and found that the pieces of three of the suits were mixed up. In June 2002, the custodians of the three suits—the National Trust of Australia, the State Library of Victoria and the Police Museum—got together and exchanged pieces so that there are now three complete original suits of armour.

Ned is reported as saying he wanted to send the train and police "to hell". There is one theory that the destruction of the police train would mark the beginning of a bold plan to take control of the government of North Eastern Victoria and that Ned planned to form a republic, with himself as leader. Another plan may have been to rally their supporters and raid a number of banks in the area. Later Ned said he had no intention of derailing the train, merely stopping it so that he could take police hostages to trade for his mother. Whatever Ned's intentions, Glenrowan was a disaster. After nearly two years on the run, the Kelly Gang had finally met its end.

Silenced

What if you were there...

The jail's quiet today. They're all listening. They want to hear the crash as the trapdoor falls. They hope to hear the crack as his neck breaks. So that they can tell their grandchildren they were there when Ned Kelly was hanged. I'm still working though. Scrubbing at these miserable prison shirts till my hands are wrinkled like prunes. Tomorrow I might be washing Ned's shirt. The one he died in. There's no clock here in the prison laundry, but I can see the sun through the one barred window – high up so that none of us women can climb out of it. My poor Ned. I reckon he's got no more than ten minutes of life left to him. I wish I could be with him to comfort him. I suppose he's remembering it all now, just like I am, wondering how it might have been different.

I keep seeing him as he was when he was a boy. Always cheerful, always ready to help. And with a way of saying things that would always have us in fits.

We had a happy home up at Greta. It wasn't much, just a wooden hut. We weren't rich. We struggled with that patch of land, but we were happy and we had each other. We were content. If the troopers had let us alone, we'd still be there today. But they wouldn't let us alone. Not for five minutes. They blamed my boys for every bit of mischief from Wallan to Wodonga. It was as if their one aim in life was to see the Kelly boys behind bars.

And the girls, they wouldn't leave them alone either. Handsome, strong-willed girls they are and there was always some trooper with his eye on one of them. They'd wake us in the middle of the night with a cock and bull story about looking for a stolen saddle. They'd turn us all out of bed and ransack the house just so they could see the girls standing shivering in their nightgowns. That snake Fitzpatrick, he was the worst of them all.

I never touched Fitzpatrick, no matter what they say. I swear before the God I will soon see, I didn't hit him. Even if I had, he was wearing his helmet. I could hardly have killed him. That's what made my Ned so angry. And then when they put me in jail, not for a few months but for three years, that was the end of it. Ned wouldn't rest until I was free. That's what turned my son into a wanted man. He would have done anything for his sisters and me.

The warder tells me thousands of people are standing outside in the street. Ghouls, I said, waiting like crows for a sick lamb to die. No, he said, sympathisers who were willing to put their names on a petition to save Ned's life. Imagine that.

It must be nearly time. I've prayed for a miracle. Nothing can save Ned now. They're all watching me, the other women, the warders, waiting for me to cry out or fall in a faint. I won't give them that satisfaction. I'll just keep scrubbing these shirts. If I shed a tear, it will mingle with the sweat and the steam. No one will know.

I hope Ned can stay strong and die like a Kelly. God knows his true nature and I pray He will forgive him his crimes and look after him as he deserves.

Mrs Ellen Kelly, Ned's mother

Captive

Ned recovered from his wounds, though his hands were crippled and his left arm useless. The police made only one charge against him, that of the murder of Thomas Lonigan at Stringybark Creek. The authorities were still afraid of Ned, even though he was safely in jail. He was kept in solitary confinement with a guard outside his cell keeping a 24-hour watch in case he tried to commit suicide. He was not allowed to have any visitors. The police made one exception to this rule – his mother was permitted to see him. It was the first time they had seen each other for almost two years.

> **It is not that I fear death; I fear it as little as to drink a cup of tea. My mind is easy as the mind of any man in this world as I am prepared to show before God and man. A day will come at a bigger court than this when we shall see which is right and which is wrong.**
>
> From Ned's trial as reported in the *Argus*, 29 October 1880

The money from the bank robberies had been spent or given away. There was no money for Ned's defence. His sisters could not raise the required money. Five months after the Glenrowan siege, Ned stood in the dock of the Supreme Court in Melbourne, his case defended by a young and inexperienced barrister whom he had never met. The young man knew less about the case than the average person. He had been out of Victoria for most of what was now known as the Kelly Outbreak.

As he stumbled through his clumsy speech, the barrister called no witnesses to defend Ned. Ned himself, a man known to be good with words, didn't say anything in his own defence. The Jerilderie Letter, in which Ned explained how he and his family had been wronged, was not read. The trial lasted less than two days.

The judge at the trial was none other than Sir Redmond Barry, the same man who had sentenced Ned's mother so severely. The jury took less than half an hour to consider their verdict. Justice Barry draped a black cloth over his head, but could not resist speaking to the famous man who had been silent throughout the trial. Ned spoke softly and clearly. He stated that he wished he had spoken in his own defence. Justice Barry pronounced the sentence: death by hanging.

There is one wish in conclusion I would like you to grant me, that is the release of my Mother before my execution as detaining her in prison could not make any difference to the Government now for the day will come when all men will be judged by their mercy and deeds...
Letter to the Governor of Victoria, 10 November 1880

Last-minute Pleas

Ned still had faith in the written word. In his cell he produced a series of three letters to the Governor of

Victoria setting forth his defence. The shoot-out with the police had left Ned with crippled hands. Unable to write, he dictated them to a prison guard.

Opinion had swung in Ned's favour again. A public meeting to save Ned's life attracted a crowd of 4000 people. Just five days before his execution his solicitor started a petition to save Ned's life. In that short time 32,000 signatures were collected. His sisters and brother walked to Government House to plead with the Governor in person. But none of these efforts were successful.

The Gallows

Ned Kelly was hanged in the Melbourne Gaol in Russell Street at 10 a.m. on 11 November 1880. He was 25 years old. He was accompanied to the gallows by a priest carrying a cross, who had just administered the last rites, and three other ministers. His mother, Ellen Kelly, in the last months of her three-year sentence for the attempted murder of Constable Fitzpatrick, was working in the women's wing of the same jail just metres from where Ned was hanged. Outside the jail a crowd of 5000 people gathered to mourn his death.

Ned's last words were reported by one journalist as "Such is life". Another newspaper said they were

"Ah well, I suppose it has come to this". Either way, Ned was calm to the last and resigned to his fate.

The hangman put the noose around Ned's neck, pulled a white execution hood over his head, strapped his arms to his side and pulled the lever which opened the trapdoor. As the priest muttered prayers, Ned fell two-and-a-half metres and was hanged by the neck.

The last photo of Ned, taken the day before he was hanged.

Grisly Deeds

After Ned's death a plaster cast of his head was made. A death mask of the executed criminal was put on display at the Bourke Street Waxworks the very next day. The death mask can still be seen in the Old Melbourne Gaol and many people who see it remark on the peaceful expression on the face.

Ned's skull was reportedly used as a paperweight on a public servant's desk until it was taken to the Old Melbourne Gaol as an exhibit. It was stolen from a glass case in the Gaol in 1978 and has never been seen since.

Ned's head was then cut off, his brain removed for scientific examination and his skull was sent to be examined by a phrenologist. But that was not the end of it. Doctors and students taking part in this post mortem examination then proceeded to take pieces of the body as souvenirs. The disfigured, headless body was then buried in the prison grounds in an unmarked grave.

Reading His Bumps

At the time of Ned's death it was believed that phrenology could prove that the size and shape of the brain was responsible for a person's personality. Phrenologists made maps of the human skull and divided them into characteristics such as pride, bravery and secretiveness. They thought that the shape and size of the "bumps" on a skull showed if the areas of the brain below were large or small. A phrenologist examined Ned's skull after he was hanged. He said that because of the large areas of self-esteem, destructiveness and love of power, it was obvious that Ned was destined for a life of crime. He particularly noted the small size of the "caution" area.

A Royal Commission

Though Ned didn't live to see it, his actions did have an effect. There was an outcry for an inquiry into the way police had handled the whole affair. Four months after Ned's execution, the Royal Commission of Enquiry into the Circumstances of the Kelly Outbreak began. Though Ned's trial had lasted for less than two days, the Royal Commission lasted for six months. This time it was the police who were on trial.

The first film made about Ned Kelly was *The Story of the Kelly Gang*, an Australian film made in 1907. It was the first feature film ever made in the world. When it was advertised they measured the length of the film in feet (4000 feet), not in minutes. Only nine minutes of the film have survived. This was unearthed from a Melbourne rubbish tip.

The Royal Commission was very critical of the police force. From the Chief Commissioner down, almost every policeman involved in the Kelly Hunt was reprimanded. Ned would have been pleased to know that all of his enemies suffered because of their bungling response to the Kelly Outbreak.

Sergeant Steele was rewarded for his part of the capture, but demoted because of his actions at the siege; Chief Commissioner Standish, who had already retired, was severely criticised for the "grave error" of reducing the number of police in Kelly Country; Superintendent Sadleir was found guilty of "errors of judgement" and demoted; Superintendents Hare and Nicolson were forced to retire; Inspector Brooke Smith, who was now a mental wreck, was declared to be lazy and incompetent and was also made to retire; the police at the Sherritt hut were found guilty of cowardice and disobeying orders. Constable Bracken was the only policeman to get any praise from the Royal Commission. The newspaper reporters on the scene at Glenrowan received more praise than the police did.

The first screenings of *The Story of the Kelly Gang* were banned by the government. They thought the story might incite people to become outlaws.

The £8000 reward was divided up among 67 people who were involved with the gang's capture at Glenrowan – most of them were policemen. The crew of the train was also rewarded. Superintendent Hare received £800 – the largest cut of the reward. Mr Curnow, the schoolteacher who stopped the train, came next with £550. He complained that this wasn't enough and the amount was raised to £1000.

No Rest

Ned's remains were buried in an unmarked grave in the grounds of the Old Melbourne Gaol. Almost 50 years later, the bodies of a number of prisoners were dug up and reburied in the grounds of Pentridge Prison. Then in 2009, the bodies were exhumed again after the closure of the prison, when work began to convert the prison to a housing estate, parklands and a business precinct.

The remains of 34 people were unearthed and many of the bones were mixed together, but there was one set of bones in a wooden box. It was an almost complete skeleton. The only piece that was missing was the skull.

Ned's last words to the trial judge, Sir Redmond Barry, after he had sentenced him to death were, "I will see you there where I go." The judge died suddenly 12 days later.

Forensic Proof

The remains were handed to the Victorian Institute of Forensic Medicine (VIFM) for identification. The investigation took 20 months. Samples of bone from all the skeletons were sent to Argentina for analysis by the EAAF (Argentine Forensic Anthropology Team). A blood sample was taken from Leigh Olver, a great-grandson of Ned's sister Ellen. His DNA was compared to the DNA from all the remains found at Pentridge. Mr Olver's DNA matched that of the skeleton found in the box.

"To think a group of scientists could identify the body of a man who was executed more than 130 years ago, moved and buried in a haphazard fashion...is amazing."
Attorney General of Victoria Robert Clark, 2011

Bullet holes were found in the bones which matched the wounds Ned had received at Glenrowan and recorded by a doctor before he was hanged. More than 130 years after his death, Ned's body had been found and identified. The news made headlines around the world.

Ned's Head

A man who had claimed for many years to have Ned's skull finally agreed to hand it over for forensic examination in 2009. DNA from the skull was compared to Mr Olver's DNA. It did not match. The skull was the one stolen from the Old Melbourne Gaol back in 1978, but it was not Ned's.

The whereabouts of Ned's skull is still a mystery.

Final Resting Place

The Victorian government returned Ned Kelly's remains to the Kelly family. On 20 January 2013, 132 years after his execution, his remains were reburied in the Greta Cemetery where his mother, brother Dan and other family members are also buried. Ned finally got his wish to be buried in consecrated ground.

> **"There is one wish in conclusion I would like you to grant me, that is the release of my mother before my execution as detaining her in prison could not make any difference to the Government...also if you would grant permission for my friends to have my body that they might bury it in consecrated ground."**
> Ned Kelly, letter to the Governor of Victoria, 10 Nov 1880.

A new headstone commemorates the Kelly burials, including Ned's, but it does not mark the site of his grave. Because of concerns that vandals might try to dig up the remains of this famous man, the grave was sealed with concrete and is unmarked.

Still Famous After All These Years

More than 200 books have been written about Ned Kelly. The first feature length film in the world was about the Kellys. Four other films about the Kelly Gang have been made and two new films are currently in planning. Many artists have made Ned and his exploits the subject of paintings and sculptures. There have been plays, TV programs, museum exhibitions – even a rock opera, a ballet and a jazz music composition. In 1980 Ned became the first criminal to be commemorated by the Australian postal service when a pre-stamped envelope featuring him was issued.

More than 120 years after his death, people are still fascinated by Ned Kelly. Though few relics remain, tourists visit Glenrowan, Euroa and Jerilderie. In the museum at the Old Melbourne Gaol, every day there are visitors who want to see the gallows where Ned was hanged. In the souvenir shop there is a selection of Ned Kelly souvenirs, including tea towels, fridge magnets and toys. It's hard to imagine what Ned would make of this, if he could see it. Probably nobody would be more amazed by his continuing fame than Ned himself.

In a country founded by convicts and poor migrants, Ned Kelly has become a symbol of the battler fighting against the odds. He was a larrikin but he had a good heart. He was a criminal but he fought against injustice and never gave up. The fact that he failed and is still considered to be a hero is a uniquely Australian sentiment.

Historians still sift though the evidence and debate the unanswered questions. Did Ned shoot Fitzpatrick? What were his plans at Glenrowan?

Was he a bad man or a saint? People will go on talking about Ned Kelly for a long time to come.

What They Said About Ned

People who were involved in the adventures of the Kelly Gang were haunted by their experiences for the rest of their lives. Speaking about the events years later, here is what some of them had to say about Ned and the Kelly Gang.

Superintendent Hare, 1894

"Ned Kelly was a flash ill-looking young blackguard... Notwithstanding all [his] boasted pluck and boasts, how game he would die etc., he was the only one who in any way showed the white feather...he begged for mercy, and asked [the police] to spare his life. There is no doubt that, had he been able to walk, he would have gone off, leaving his comrades behind in the hotel."

Samuel Gill, editor of Jerilderie newspaper, 1910

"The raid on the bank at Jerilderie was skilfully designed, every detail having been carefully thought out. The plot laid to trap the police and gain possession of the police-station was the work of no ordinary mind."

Constable Fitzpatrick, 1911

"Ned Kelly rises before me as I speak. Considering his environment, he was a superior man. He possessed great natural ability, and under favourable circumstances would probably have become a leader of men in good society, instead of the head of a gang of outlaws."

Mrs Kelly, 1911

"Think what the police have done to me and mine, and then tell me if you wonder that the boys turned and smote the ones who had so persecuted them. If they had been trying to provoke the boys to break the law and retaliate, they could not have done more than they did, and I firmly believe they were trying."

Mrs Jones, owner of Glenrowan Inn, 1911

"I well remember Kelly coming to my place that dreadful night... [He] said he would shoot me if I refused to do everything that he told me... Ned Kelly was most cruel to all of us that day. He said if he could see his way to burn down the house and those who set the police onto him, he'd do it."

Patrick Allen, storekeeper at Benalla, 1911

"They were good fellows apart from their crimes. And they would have made splendid soldiers. It's a pity they got a bad start."

Detective Ward, 1911

"After the battle, Ned Kelly was lying under guard at the railway station. He said it was Jones' whisky that killed them... He never forgot a good turn. I let him off in Wangaratta once when I should have arrested him... He never forgot that."

Superintendent Sadleir, 1913

"The true picture of a bushranger shows him as a very poor and sordid thing indeed. The Kellys, in spite of a few successful enterprises, were as poor and unheroic as any of their kind."

Constable Richards of Euroa, 1931

"He was a bushranger but he was the gamest man I ever saw."

1841	Ned's father, Red Kelly, is transported from Ireland
1851	
1852	
1853	
1854	Ned is born, December
1855	
1865	
1866	Ned rescues a drowning boy Ned's father dies, December
1867	First brush with the law, May
1868	
1869	Ned becomes Harry Power's apprentice
1870	First jail sentence—for violent assault, November 1870 – March 1871
1871	Second jail sentence—for receiving a stolen horse, August 1871 – February 1874
1872	
1873	
1874	Ned's honest years, 1874 – 1877
1875	
1876	
1877	Cattle stealing with stepfather George King
1878	The Fitzpatrick Affair, April Ned's mother, Ellen Kelly, is jailed, October The shootings at Stringybark Creek, October The Kelly Gang are declared outlaws, November The Kelly Gang rob a bank in Euroa, December Ned writes the Cameron Letter, December
1879	The Kelly Gang rob a bank in Jerilderie, February Ned writes the Jerilderie Letter, February The reward for their capture, dead or alive, is raised to £8000, February
1880	Joe Byrne shoots Aaron Sherritt dead, June The Kelly Gang's last stand at the Glenrowan Inn. Dan Kelly, Joe Byrne and Steve Hart are killed, June Ned is sentenced to death, October Ned is hanged at the Old Melbourne Gaol, November

Acknowledgements

There are many differing versions of the story of the Kelly Gang. For the sequence of events in my book I have mainly used the books *Ned Kelly: A Short Life* by Ian Jones and *Ned Kelly: The Authentic Illustrated History* by Keith McMenomy as references. I am indebted to these historians for their years of thorough and dedicated research starting at a time when research was much more difficult than it is today and important documents were hidden in the depths of the Public Record Office Victoria.

My task in researching the Kelly story for this book was easy: the Public Record Office Victoria has put the key Kelly documents on the Internet; the newspapers of the day are all on microfilm; at the time I was writing, the Old Melbourne Gaol staged the biggest Ned Kelly exhibition ever put together; the careful referencing of Mr Jones and Mr McMenomy led me to important newspaper items and less obvious books.

I would like to take this opportunity to thank Mr Jones, Mr McMenomy, the Public Record Office Victoria, the National Trust of Australia and the staff at the State Library of Victoria for making the research for this book a pleasurable and stress-free experience.

Internet sites

The Victorian Public Records Office has a large collection of Kelly documents.

There is an online description of the collection with links to digital images at
http://prov.vic.gov.au/whats-on/exhibitions/ned-kelly

The State Library of Victoria has a collection of Kelly images which you can view online through the catalogue at
http://search.slv.vic.gov.au
Type Ned Kelly in the search box and select Pictures from the *I want to search* drop-down menu.

There is a link to a digitised version of the Jerilderie Letter at
http://slv.vic.gov.au/our-collections/treasures-curios/jerilderie-letter
Also if you can visit the State Library of Victoria, Ned's armour and a page or two from the original Jerilderie Letter are on permanent display as part of the free exhibition *The Changing Face of Victoria* in the Dome Gallery.

There are many websites about Ned. One that has a lot of resources, including a digital archive of newspaper articles is the *Ned Kelly Australian Iron Outlaw* website.
www.ironoutlaw.com

The Victorian Institute of Forensic Medicine website has detailed information about the identification of Ned's body.
http://www.vifm.org/forensics/the-ned-kelly-project/

Sources

Walker Books acknowledges the assistance of the Victorian Police Historical Unit; Matt Shore at *Ned: The Exhibition*; the State Library of Victoria; the Public Record Office Victoria; and private collectors for allowing us to reprint the following images in *Black Snake: The daring of Ned Kelly*.

Page 23 Ned in boxing trunks: Private Collection

Page 34 Constable Alexander Fitzpatrick: Victorian Police Historical Unit

Page 40 Dan Kelly: La Trobe Picture Collection, State Library of Victoria

Page 41 Joe Byrne: Private Collection

Page 41 Steve Hart: La Trobe Picture Collection, State Library of Victoria

Page 50 The clearing at Stringybark Creek: Victorian Police Historical Unit

Page 76 Plain-clothed policemen involved in the hunt for the Kelly Gang: Victorian Police Historical Unit

Page 90 £8000 Reward Poster: Victorian Police Historical Unit

Page 103 Armour made by Kelly Gang: La Trobe Picture Collection, State Library of Victoria

Reproduced with the permission of the Keeper of Public Records, Public Record Office Victoria, Australia:

Pages 2, 14, 21 PROV VPRS 4966/P Kelly Historical Collection, Unit 1

Cover PROV VPRS 937/P Inward Registered Correspondence, Unit 272

Page 119 PROV VPRS 515/P Central Register of Male Prisoners, Unit 17

Index